THOMAS JEFFERSON

A Well-Tempered Mind

Also by CARL BINGER

Revolutionary Doctor: *Benjamin Rush (1746–1813)*
The Two Faces of Medicine
The Doctor's Job
More About Psychiatry
Personality in Arterial Hypertension
(*with others*)
Post Meridian

Portrait (1791) by Charles Willson Peale (Courtesy of Independence
National Historical Park Collection, Philadelphia)

THOMAS JEFFERSON

A Well-Tempered Mind

by CARL BINGER

W · W · NORTON & COMPANY · INC ·
NEW YORK

Dedicated to

Stanley Cobb

Friend of more than sixty years

ACKNOWLEDGMENTS

When one writes a book, one usually assumes various debts of gratitude which can be repaid with words of thanks only. To list all those who have helped me would be a large undertaking. I begin with the libraries, Widener and Houghton at Harvard, the Boston Athenaeum, and the library of the Massachusetts Historical Society.

Beyond these, there are several individuals to whom I owe much for their help. Two of my younger colleagues at the Harvard University Health Services, Dr. Randolph Catlin and Dr. Preston K. Munter, read the manuscript in an earlier version and gave me the benefit of their good taste and critical judgment. Dr. Michael T. McGuire of the Massachusetts General Hospital took pains to write a careful commentary which led to the final revision. I am especially indebted to him, as I am again to my associate, Miss Marjorie E. Sprague, for her editorial help and for putting the manuscript in presentable form.

Mr. Peter Wood, Allston Burr Senior Tutor in Eliot House at Harvard, read the manuscript for historical accuracy and caught several minor errors which I should have overlooked without his help.

As I did in my book on Benjamin Rush, I turned again to Dr. Lyman H. Butterfield, well-known historiographer, for his comments. From these I profited greatly. They led to a shortening and tightening of the text, but he did not see the book in its final form and is therefore not responsible for its present contents. Lewis Mumford, whom I greatly admire for his wisdom and his art, gave me the benefit of both, and for these I am much in his debt. My old friend Storer B. Lunt, former president of W. W. Norton & Company, took precious time from his retirement to make valuable comments.

Thanks also go to my son and two daughters for suffering me to read parts of the manuscript of this book aloud to them from time to time. But I want to thank especially my wife, who helped immeasurably, lending a willing and encouraging ear at all times —even the most inopportune.

The following publishers generously granted permission to quote from the works indicated:

Coward-McCann, Inc., Marie Kimball, *Jefferson, the Road to Glory.* Copyright 1943 by Coward-McCann.

Doubleday & Company, Inc., John Dos Passos, *The Head and the Heart,* copyright 1954 by John Dos Passos. Reprinted by permission of Doubleday & Company, Inc.

Harcourt Brace Jovanovich, Inc., Clinton Rossiter, *Alexander Hamilton and the Constitution;* Saul K. Padover, *Jefferson.*

Little, Brown and Company, Dumas Malone, *Jefferson and His Time.* 4 vols.

The Nock Estate, Albert Jay Nock, *Jefferson.*

Oxford University Press, Merrill D. Peterson, *The Jefferson Image in the American Mind.*

THOMAS JEFFERSON

A Well-Tempered Mind

FOREWORD

❧ ❦

I intend in this book to review part of Jefferson's life and, without suppressing any contrary evidence, to try to bring out those salient facts that go to establish the existence of his well-tempered mind: a mind distinguished by its inner harmony and by a happy reconciliation of opposites. Of these, perhaps the most telling elements are the masculine and feminine, combined as they were in Jefferson to release his singular creativeness. This fortunate mingling of opposites is no mere compromise but an unconscious process that results in the formation of something new—in itself, a high act of creation.

The reader will recognize how rare a possession such a well-balanced mind is. He will not, I hope, confuse it with a "normal" mind. *Normal* signifies, in one sense, statistically average. According to this meaning, no one would call Jefferson's endowments normal, but in the other and Platonic sense of *normal* as *ideal,* perhaps Jefferson's mind could in most respects be called normal. It is probable that some of his intellectual energy and curiosity were reactions to an underlying depression and to his exquisite sensitivity, but these attributes are certainly not abnormal in a genius. It is genius itself that is statistically abnormal. The fact of the appearance of such a mind among us should sharpen our aims and raise our spirits, even if it is not given to every man to bend the bow of Ulysses.

Although I shall in the main restrict myself to a few decades in telling my story, I shall have to spill over these limits in order to make this account revealing. It would be foolish to truncate this biographical sketch arbitrarily; but, in the main, it will extend from Jefferson's birth in 1743 through the succeeding decades until he was elected president in 1800.

The years between thirty and fifty are the critical ones in most men's lives. This statement, however, needs to be qualified. The rate and degree and quality of a man's development are variable in both pace and direction, depending on many circumstances, not the least of which is chance. At fifty, most men will have accomplished much of their life's work, or at least will have made their meaningful contributions. This statement also needs qualification. The rate of a man's development and maturation is extraordinarily variable, depending on his genetic composition and also on those influences in his immediate environment that press upon him and help to shape him. Cervantes wrote *Don Quixote* after sixty; and the best rosarian I have known was a practicing lawyer until he was past sixty, when he had a "nervous breakdown" and was told to "take it easy and get a hobby." He became an expert, a world-famous breeder of roses who developed many new varieties.

Human beings with extraordinary vitality will always astound us. Perhaps this is why Thomas Jefferson remains such an elusive figure. He is not easily cribbed and cabined. When we think that we really understand him, he reveals some new side to us and displays his superlative strength and versatility. This very quality has made him suspect and the object of much criticism, even contumely, from the more pedestrian among us.

In 1767, at twenty-four, Jefferson was introduced to the practice of the law at the General Court of Virginia by his loyal friend and mentor, George Wythe. Although Jefferson had said of himself that he was bred to the law, the law never could quite contain him. It gave him a view of the dark side of humanity, but he turned to poetry and to his intense love of nature to brighten his life. The lawyer's trade, he said, "is to question everything, yield nothing, and talk by the hour." * (He had even more caustic things to say about his medical confrères; for example, that when he saw two or three doctors huddled in consultation, he always looked overhead for a turkey buzzard.)

In the first year of his practice of the law, Jefferson was employed in sixty-eight cases. Within two years the number had risen threefold. But this does not reflect the whole amount of his business, only that done in connection with the General Court. In addition, he was retained as attorney or counsel in as many as 430 cases in the year 1771. His earnings gradually mounted in three years to a little above £420. In view of the low rate of legal fees then paid in Virginia, this showed him to have been a highly successful young lawyer. Further evidence is provided by the character of his clients, who included the Blands, the Burwells, the Byrds, and also the Careys, Carters, Lees, Nelsons, Pages, and Randolphs, most of the great names of the Virginia aristocracy.

The law was then an aristocratic profession, and the men who practiced it in Virginia were distinguished in the main for their erudition, if not for their fortunes. Thomas Jefferson was by natural endowment and by training qualified to be the outstanding lawyer that he became. His extraordinary diligence in collecting and collating facts and in hunting for precedents through stacks of legal tomes equipped him superbly to prepare cases for trial. But as a barrister his voice lacked the volume, the timbre, and the resonance to make a telling impression. If he spoke louder than in an ordinary conversational tone, his voice soon became husky and seemed to "sink in his throat." Perhaps this is why he never became an accomplished advocate in court, much less a gifted orator. He seldom spoke before legislative or popular assemblies. Whether the difficulty with his voice was due to some anatomical defect in his larynx or his sinuses, or to some emotional inhibition, it is impossible to say, but since a clear and ringing voice is so often the hallmark of courage and trust in one's self, one might guess from Jefferson's feeble voice that he lacked these attributes —at least when called upon to display them in public.

Perhaps his mind was too mathematical and precise to express itself freely in unguarded spoken words without the inherent cen-

* See Notes, page 199.

sorship permitted by the use of a pen. But I doubt that this characteristic would explain his inhibitions. As an "office lawyer" he had few equals in the commonwealth; he possessed all the necessary ingredients to make him one. Not least was his habit of getting everything on paper in an orderly and systematic way, so that his great store of knowledge was always available to him. Added to this was his power to state a case with such clearness and economy that argument often became superfluous.

One might justifiably conclude from this sketch that Jefferson possessed some of the earmarks of what we have come to call an obsessive-compulsive personality: great industry and perseverance; a meticulous interest in the proper and judicious use of words; care in his personal expenditures, accounting often for the last penny. But at the same time, we find him aesthetically responsive and open to the tenderness and beauty of nature, of women, and of children. It is foolish indeed to try to typecast him, or for that matter, any genius.

That he was a genius there seems little question, even if the judgment rests only on his stupendous industry and versatility. Early in life he had a clear notion of his own character and proper role. In his mature years he said of himself: "When I first entered on the stage of public life (now twenty-four years ago), I came to a resolution never to engage, while in public office, in any kind of enterprise for improvement of my fortune, nor to wear any other character than that of farmer." This resolution, as he said, made him richer in contentment than he would have been with an increase of fortune.

On the Fourth of July 1826, Thomas Jefferson's eyes closed in the final slumber of death. He was then in his eighty-fourth year, and the republic over whose destiny he had recently presided was but fifty years old. A fact less generally known than it should be is that Jefferson and John Adams, who was eight years older, died on the same memorable day within a few hours of each other. A month later an English journal, *John Bull*, carried this notice:

"By a curious coincidence, Adams and Jefferson, two of the revolted colonists, who signed the Declaration of American Independence, died on the 4th of July, that being the fiftieth anniversary of their *rebellious triumph* over their mother country. This coincidence is, however, rendered less curious by a statement which has reached us, that these patriarch *malcontents* brought on their sympathetic deaths by too liberal *potations* in honor of their unnatural gratitude."

This characteristic coloring of news is obviously no new device —either in England or in this country. Both of these patriots were notably abstemious—especially Jefferson, who drank light wines only and could hardly be persuaded to swallow a little brandy in his final illness. (John Adams drank hard cider occasionally.)

Thomas Jefferson faced his end, as he had his life, with equanimity and cheerfulness. To his grandson, Thomas Jefferson Randolph, he said, "Do not imagine for a moment that I feel the smallest solicitude about the result; I am like an old watch, with a pinion worn out here, and a wheel there, until it can go no longer."

His death and John Adams's on the Fourth of July were perhaps no curious coincidence, but an example of "historical inevitability." Their wheels had come full turn, their work accomplished, and in a sense they had nothing more to live for. Men often die under such circumstances when they no longer feel tethered to the world. The date of their deaths was in itself a kind of celebration, an avowal of their belief in all they had fought for and suffered. John Adams's dying words were indeed prophetic ones, "Thomas Jefferson still survives!" James Madison, perhaps Jefferson's closest friend, who succeeded him as president, had written in a letter addressed to Dr. Robley Dunglinson, Jefferson's physician, on July 6, 1826, "I never doubted that the last scene of our illustrious friend would be worthy of the life it closed."

This was a life of enormous industry, of the tenderest affections, of disappointment and frustration, of heartache and tragedy, of rigorous discipline and self-control, of joy and merriment and love, and of the most intense aesthetic satisfaction, all balanced in well-tempered harmony. Such traits are partly inborn, partly the result of early influences, partly cultivated through long practice. One cannot come much closer than this combination in assigning their origins.

In reviewing the life of this great man, we encounter several repetitive themes and conflicts, as, for example, between his need to be strong and his passive dependent needs. All his life he looked for the moral support of a strong man with which, in his youth, his father had so richly supplied him. This search, however, often failed him, as in the cases of Patrick Henry and Alexander Hamilton. But, from Washington, Madison, Monroe, and Lafayette he got the support that he craved.

Throughout his life we can recognize his wish to return home and to run for cover. After each term of office, he habitually refused to stand for election again. Instead, we see him passively waiting in the wings for the presidency. The early termination of his marriage, because of his wife's untimely death, forced him into a feminine role, expressed in his tender care of his daughters and the children of his widowed sister, and also in the aesthetic and artistic joys of life in Paris. He was perhaps his happiest while traveling alone in France, which spoke directly to this feminine side of him.

I have not intended to equate *feminine* with weakness or passivity—far from it. I have wished rather to stress Jefferson's aesthetic and care-taking attributes, and these, for the sake of convenience, I have called feminine. His more aggressive and executive characteristics and his extraordinary precision of mind, again for the sake of convenience, I have called masculine.

CHAPTER ONE

❧ ❧

Thomas Jefferson was fortunate in his parentage. The Jeffersons were of Welsh origin and came to America from near Mount Snowden in the early 1600s. By 1619 one of them sat in the Virginia House of Burgesses, the first such body to be convened on this continent and the first to establish the fact that by migrating to America the colonists had lost none of their rights as Englishmen. They were of stalwart yeoman stock, belonging to that class of free men, intermediate between squire and tenant, who owned and worked their own land. This tradition of independent self-reliance was bred in the bone, and all his life Thomas Jefferson favored a society of self-sufficing free farmers. They were the men who made America great.

The first ancestor of whom Thomas had any particular information was his grandfather, Thomas, who, with the help of a few slaves, had cleared and taken up a tract of land in Chesterfield, Virginia, to the west of the tobacco country. This Thomas had three sons: Thomas, who died young; Field, who settled on the waters of the Roanoke; and Peter, our Thomas's father. Peter was born in about 1707 or 1708. He grew into a man of prodigious strength, as if hewn out of live oak, and single-handedly experienced the naked truth of the wilderness. As a younger son, he looked forward to little in the way of inheritance, but he learned the art of surveying, which amounted to a kind of liberal profession in a new country. When surveying in the wilderness, he could tire out his slaves and his mules and continue till nightfall, and when his work was finished he would sleep in the hollow of a tree to the accompaniment of the howling of wolves.

"My father's education," wrote Jefferson, "had been quite neglected; but being of a strong mind, sound judgment, and eager after information, he read much and improved himself." He had not only a thirst for knowledge but also great energy of character. He cherished a worn edition of Shakespeare; and he left to his descendants, among his books, copies of *The Spectator* and some volumes of Swift and Pope as well.

When Peter Jefferson was thirty-one, he married Jane Randolph, the nineteen-year-old daughter of Isham Randolph, who traced his pedigree far back in England and Scotland, a lineage of good breeding that Thomas Jefferson was later inclined to dismiss as being of no special importance, but which probably lent him some awareness of his superiority, of which he seems to have been conscious. All his life he was prouder of his simpler, self-reliant democratic Jefferson blood than of that of the privileged Randolphs. They were of the Virginia aristocracy and occupied a noble mansion on the James attended by a hundred servants, both blacks and indentured whites. The lowland aristocracy clung to the manners of the cultivated landed gentry of the mother country. Peter, by contrast, surveyed and cleared a thousand acres of land in Albemarle County, on the Rivanna River where it passes through the southwest passage. This tract lay mostly on the bottom land, but it extended up into the hills, including the land later to be named Monticello. With his own hands, he built himself a plain, weather-boarded house. The third or fourth settler in that part of the country, his other neighbors were the hostile Monacans and Tuscaroras. Since there was no suitable site for a house on his property, Peter obtained, in exchange for a large bowl of arrack punch, an additional four hundred acres from his close friend Colonel William Randolph, the younger proprietor of Tuckahoe, who was Isham's nephew and his future wife's cousin. To this house he brought his rich, gentle, and well-born bride. The place was called Shadwell, after the parish in England in which Jane had been born.

In the service of the crown, Peter Jefferson surveyed the boundary line between Virginia and North Carolina and drew the first map of Virginia that was not purely conjectural. Not only the county surveyor and a county colonel in the army, but also a justice of the peace, a vestryman of the Episcopal church and a burgess as well, he remained, in spite of his comfortable station in life, a Whig and a thorough democrat. He was at home in the wild frontier beauty of the Blue Ridge, so different from the ample, gently spreading tidewater demesne of the Tory Randolphs, who led lives of hospitable and sophisticated elegance.

The fusion of these two strains gave rise to Thomas Jefferson. Probably more than anything else, this accounted for his genius, for what I have called his well-tempered mind, the harmonious meeting and blending of opposites.

He was born at Shadwell, about five miles east of Charlottesville, on April 13, 1743, the third child, but first son, after three years of marriage. Then followed seven more children; of these, two sons died in infancy. The rest were all girls, except for Randolph, a much younger brother, whose twin sister also died as an infant. Thomas's brother Randolph lived to the age of sixty but seems to have accomplished relatively little in his lifetime.

Perhaps the order of birth was partly responsible for the difference in the two brothers. In keeping with the English tradition, great value was set on the first-born son; primogeniture was the law in the colonies until Jefferson himself was instrumental in its abolishment. Primogeniture alone would have led his father to invest much time and interest and love in his elder male child; moreover, Randolph was only two years old when his father died, and not yet ripe for his companionship. But there may have been genetic influences as well to account for the contrast between the brothers. No two brothers are made of the same stuff. Each inherits his own particular pattern or mosaic of genes; and these go far towards determining not only his size and shape and coloring, but also his temperament and his intellectual capabilities.

Thomas Jefferson was fortunate both in his genetic composition and in the happy forces that molded him. He was closely identified with his father, who influenced him mightily. He gave Thomas his first religious instruction, taught him to say his prayers, to read the Bible, and to be diligent in his studies, emphasizing especially the importance of the classics. Thomas Jefferson was eternally grateful for this. Much later in life, when a mature man, he wrote: "I thank on my knees, Him who directed my early education, for having put into my possession this rich source of delight; and I would not exchange it for anything which I could then have acquired. . . ."

Peter Jefferson also taught his son to shoot deer and wild turkey and to paddle a canoe on the Rivanna. He made an expert horseman of Thomas, so that later in life Thomas Jefferson and George Washington were regarded as the finest horsemen of their time. But precious beyond all these gifts was that of almost perfect health bequeathed by father to son. There was a striking physical resemblance between them. Both were erect, powerful, agile, and robust. Even into old age Thomas Jefferson was able to read without glasses and, unlike his greatly revered Washington, kept all his teeth. When he could no longer walk, he went for a hard ride, even within three weeks of his death at the age of eighty-three. But he believed that at best "a horse gives but a kind of half-exercise," and he wondered whether "we have not lost more than we have gained by the use of this animal. No one has occasioned so much the degeneracy of the human body." What would he have said to the automobile and the gradual atrophy of our organs of locomotion! As for driving, he believed that "a carriage is no better than a cradle." Walking he regarded as the best form of exercise, and with this opinion modern medical teaching would on the whole agree. He recommended the practice of carrying a gun on walks, saying, "While this gives a moderate exercise to the body, it gives boldness, enterprise and independence to the mind." "Games played with ball, and others of that nature," he thought, "are too violent for the body, and stamp no character on the mind." Health, he was convinced, is worth more than learning. All his life he distrusted drugs and coddling and was persuaded that at least two hours of hard exercise every day were "the sovereign invigorator of the body." This rigorous philosophy worked well for Jefferson, as it had for his father; but there were slighter, asthenic men, such as his friend James Madison, who probably would have succumbed had they followed this practice.

As justice of the peace, Colonel Peter Jefferson was frequently called upon to settle disputes among his neighbors, which included those between the white settlers and the Indians. The house at Shadwell was near the public highway and was frequently the stopping place for passersby, including some of the great Indian chiefs. These Indians held Peter Jefferson in high respect, for he neither feared them nor ever deceived them. One chief in particular, Ontasseté, the warrior and orator of the Cherokees, made a lasting impression on young Thomas. Ontasseté was a familiar guest on his travels to and from Williamsburg, where the Indians went frequently and in great numbers to the seat of government. On one occasion the boy was in the camp of this chief when Ontasseté made his farewell address to his people before departing for England. Seventy years later Jefferson described this memorable scene in a letter to John Adams, in 1812:

"The moon was in full splendor, and to her he seemed to address himself in his prayers for his own safety on the voyage, and that of his people during his absence; his sounding voice, distinct articulation, animated action, and the solemn silence of his people at their several fires, filled me with awe and veneration, although I did not understand a word he uttered."

Jefferson's interest in the Indians began in his boyhood and lasted for the rest of his life. For thirty years he collected their vocabularies, more than fifty of them. He planned to have them printed in collateral columns, for purposes of comparison not only with each other but with Russian, to which he found some striking resemblance. But this work was to come to naught when the trunk in which it was packed for shipping by water from Washington was broken into en route and the whole of its contents dumped into the James River. Only a few badly defaced pages were retrieved from the mud. Jefferson kept them with the hope of making another attempt at this study, but he felt himself too old to be able to make much progress in it.

His principal interest in making this comparative study was to trace the origins of the American aborigines. In his *Notes on Virginia,* he says, for example, that the Powhatans, Mannahoacs, and Monacans spoke languages so radically different from one another that interpreters were necessary when they transacted business with each other, although they all lived near the headwaters of the Potomac and Rappahannock, or on the upper reaches of the James River. Each tribe apparently spoke the language of the nation to which it was attached. A separation into dialects may be the work of a relatively short time, Jefferson believed; but "for two dialects to recede from one another till they have lost all vestiges of their common origin, must require an immense course of time; perhaps not less than many people give to the age of the earth." From this argument Jefferson figured that the red men of America were of greater antiquity than those of Asia. He thought that three different stocks existed initially and that these were separated into many little independent societies, since they had never submitted to coercive power. Their only control were their manners and the moral sense of right and wrong which was part of their nature. He found that crimes were very rare among them, and he raised the thoughtful question "whether no law as among the savage Americans, or too much law, as among civilized Europeans submits man to the greater evil." Jefferson had witnessed both conditions of existence. He was convinced that no law is preferable to too much, and that sheep are happier by themselves than under the care of wolves.

On at least two occasions during his presidency, Jefferson spoke to assemblages of Indians. The first time (1801) he addressed them as "Brothers and friends of the Miamis, Powtewatamies, and Weeauks." With great tact and sincerity he said that white men and red men were created by the same Great Spirit and were living in the same land as brothers of the same family. "The evils which of necessity encompass the life of man are sufficiently numerous. Why should we add to them by voluntarily distressing and destroying one another?" Peace, he said, is better than war. In a long and bloody war we lose many friends and gain nothing. He promised to be just and generous toward them and to help them meet the difficulties brought on by their changed circumstances.

He looked forward to seeing them cultivate the earth, raise herds of useful animals and spin and weave for their clothing; these resources were certain, he said, and would never disappoint them, whereas hunting might fail and would only expose their women and children to the miseries of hunger and cold.

Five years later he addressed the chiefs of the Cherokee nation and praised them for their industry and husbandry, saying: "My children, it is unnecessary for me to advise you against spending all your time and labor in warring with and destroying your fellow-men, and wasting your own members. You already see the folly and iniquity of it. Your young men, however, are not yet sufficiently sensible of it. Some of them cross the Mississippi to go and destroy people who have never done them an injury. My children, this is wrong and must not be; if we permit them to cross the Mississippi to war with the Indians on the other side of that river, we must let those Indians cross the river to take revenge on you. I say again, this must not be. The Mississippi now belongs to us. It must not be a river of blood. . . . .

"My children, this is what I wished to say to you. To go on in learning to cultivate the earth and to avoid war."

In his second inaugural address he stated that, in spite of the Indians' ardent love of liberty and independence, and their wish to be left undisturbed, they had been pushed by a stream of overflowing population from other regions, "within limits too narrow for the hunter's state." He spoke of the difficulties of enlightening them because of the habits of their bodies and the prejudices of their minds, and their ignorance and pride and the anti-philosophy of those whose only interest was to keep things in their present state. But he said that the Indians were being liberally furnished with implements of husbandry and household use and provided with instructors in these arts.

All his life Jefferson kept his strong sense of commiseration with the Indians. Their gradual extermination in America he saw as an extension of the brutal, unprincipled policy of England both in her Asian colonies and in Ireland, and "wherever else

Anglo-mercantile cupidity can find a twopenny interest in deluging the earth with human blood."

His concern with the Indians was one of the many interests traceable to the influence of his powerful, devout, disciplined, and magnanimous father. But he himself added, as he did indeed to everything he touched in his life, his own inordinate curiosity and need to learn.

In his *Autobiography* he gives a scant account of his schooling: "He [father] placed me at the English school at five years of age; and at the Latin at nine, where I continued until his death. My teacher, Mr. Douglas, a clergyman from Scotland, with the rudiments of the Latin and Greek languages, taught me the French; and on the death of my father, I went to the Reverend Mr. Maury, a correct classical scholar, with whom I continued two years; and then, to wit, in the spring of 1760, went to William and Mary College, where I continued two years."

As a boy, it was Homer and Virgil that he read on his canoe trips down the Rivanna. His early exposure to the classics not only filled him with delight but added that balance to his mind which was to become so much a part of him, and undoubtedly contributed greatly to his gifts as a writer of his own tongue.

Peter Jefferson died at the age of fifty, on August 17, 1757. Thomas was fourteen, and one can only guess what the loss must have meant to the son. His widowed mother was left also with six daughters and an infant son to care for. Many years later Jefferson wrote in a letter to his grandson and namesake, Thomas Jefferson Randolph:

"When I recollect that at fourteen years of age the whole care and direction of myself was thrown on myself entirely, without a relative or friend qualified to advise or guide me, and recollect the various sorts of bad company with which I associated from time to time, I am astonished that I did not turn off with some of them, and become as worthless to society as they were."

It is no reflection on his mother for him to have said that there was no one qualified to advise or guide him. A healthy adolescent boy of fourteen, so closely identified with his father, finding himself surrounded by females on all sides, will have little truck with what he regards as mere women, and will quickly cut the last shreds of apron strings, if they ever did bind him. We have no knowledge of his infancy and early childhood, but he must have been given love and tenderness to have been able to give so much of these to others. There was always a coolness about him and perhaps a fear of letting his feelings go, especially with women, to whose charms he was so susceptible. Perhaps he was even more dependent on them than most men, but he knew that real happiness could not be attained through indifference or impulsive behavior.

There are a few sparse early memories, important, perhaps, only because he recorded them. When Thomas was not more than two, his father moved to Tuckahoe, and Thomas recollected being handed up, on this occasion, to a slave on horseback, by whom he was carried on a pillow for a long distance. One can draw no inference from this memory alone, although it suggests a continued awareness of his dependent needs in spite of his self-reliance. Another memory is not too far removed from this. At five, impatient for his school to be out, he knelt behind the house and there repeated the Lord's Prayer, hoping thereby to hurry up the desired hour; and at another time he resorted to this ritual in order to allay his hunger when dinner was delayed.

The enduring bond that existed between Jefferson and his father should not be looked upon as evidence that his mother's influence was unimportant to him. Jane Jefferson was an agreeable, intelligent woman, educated, as the other Virginia ladies of high rank were, and, like them, notable as a housekeeper. She was, moreover, high-spirited, lively, cheerful, affectionate, and humorous, given to letter-writing, which she did readily and well. These traits can be found in her son. At the time of his father's death, Thomas was at an age when it was natural for a boy to try to emulate his father. This was fortunate, but the warm, tender, outgoing character of his mother seems to have left its happy traces as well, and to have given him a fundamental feeling of trust that was to endure throughout his life. If he is relatively silent about her, this can be explained more by a certain shyness in him, and a reserve when speaking of family affairs outside his family, than by any lack of responsiveness or affection. Or perhaps he was too dependent on her and had to assert his manliness by cutting himself off from her.

Both parents belonged to the Church of England, and in this church he and his brother and sisters were baptized in their infancy. He retained a lifetime "familiarity with the Bible, with the prayers and collects of the noble liturgy of the Church, and with its psalms and hymns." But in this, as in all else, he was free and unbound. His fundamental belief was in the innate morality of man. The moral sense, he thought, is as much a part of man as his arm or leg and as much a part of his nature as the senses of hearing, seeing, and feeling. Man is destined for society, he believed, and so his morality is intimately bound to his relationship with others. This belief formed the basis of Jefferson's personal ethic and of his political philosophy.

CHAPTER TWO

❧⧉❧

After his father died, Thomas moved to the school of the Reverend Mr. Maury, fourteen miles from Shadwell. His father had left directions that his oldest son was to receive a thorough classical education. Mr. Maury was described as a zealous and exact teacher and an elegant classical scholar; his pupil, in turn, was "singularly amiable and correct in his habits," and his proficiency far outran his years. This conjunction between Jefferson and Maury was a happy one. Later in life Jefferson's grandson reported that he had often heard his grandfather say "that if he had to decide between the pleasure derived from the classical education which his father had given him, and the estate left him, he would decide in favor of the former."

When he had been two years with Mr. Maury, Thomas Jefferson returned home—a tall, lanky, reddish-haired youth of sixteen, inordinately fond of walking as his favorite form of outdoor exercise, and also of playing the violin, at which he was already fairly proficient.

Within the year, he wrote his guardian, Mr. John Harvey, proposing that he should go to college. He gave as his reasons his desire to enrich his mind in mathematics as well as in the classics; also the fact that his absence from Shadwell would in large measure reduce the housekeeping expenses of the estate by putting a stop to so much company.

Accordingly, in 1760, at seventeen, he entered an advanced class at the College of William and Mary, located in Williamsburg.

Nearly a half-century later he wrote his grandson:

"From the circumstances of my position, I was often thrown into the society of horse racers, card players, fox hunters, scientific and professional men; of dignified men; and many a time have I asked myself in the enthusiastic moment of the death of a fox, the victory of a favorite horse, the issue of a question eloquently argued at the bar, or in the great council of the nation, Well which of these kinds of reputation should I prefer? That of a horse jockey? a fox hunter? an orator? or the honest advocate of my country's rights? Be assured, . . . that these little returns into ourselves, this self catechising habit is not trifling nor useless, but leads to the prudent selection and steady pursuit of what is right."

The president of the college was then the Reverend Thomas Dawson, whose faculty was copiously supplied with other sober-faced reverend gentlemen, all full of intrigue and dissensions, to the point of driving their chief to drink—a weakness Dawson readily admitted to. The town was small and boasted not more than two hundred one-story houses and a population of about one thousand whites and blacks. There were no sidewalks and no sewers. In spite of its diminutive size, it was the political and cultural center of Virginia. The college consisted of not more than three or four buildings. Although a provincial, frontier community, Williamsburg was not without its veneer of elegance. Along Duke of Gloucester Street stood some fine residences and the now famous Bruton Parish Church; at one end was the college and at the other the capitol. Nearby was the governor's palace. There was also a scattering of taverns. Drunkards were common, among them, as has been said, the president of the college. Betting on horses and other forms of gambling, including cockfighting, were openly practiced. The royalist Governor Fauquier, whom Jefferson was later to describe as the ablest man who ever filled that office, was a devotee of the gaming table. Although Jefferson was no prig, he never used tobacco, played cards, or fought, and he seldom drank. But there was a joyous, gay, fun-loving streak in his nature. Not handsome in a conventional way, he was a lean, bony, rough-hewn, and broad-shouldered youth, with a long, thin neck, a square firm jaw, a wide-winged nose "somewhat feminine and inquisitive," and very soft hazel eyes. His conversational voice was low and well-modulated. On occasion he could be high-spirited and lively and rather partial to dancing and flirting with pretty girls. Usually not very careful of his appearance, for a while at least he affected flowered waistcoats and silk stockings and carried a laced hat under his arm.

With his quick precocious intuitions, he found models in his society on whom he could pattern himself and from whose company he greatly profited. One of these was another Scotsman, Dr. William Small, his professor of mathematics, who shortly after Jefferson's arrival at college became also the interim professor of philosophy and was the first to give regular lectures in ethics, rhetoric, and belles lettres. Sixty years later Jefferson described him as "a man profound in most of the useful branches of science, with a happy talent of communication, correct and gentlemanly manners, and an enlarged and liberal mind." His young student's rare abilities were not lost on him. Even when not engaged in school work, Professor Small made Jefferson his daily companion, and from his conversation, Jefferson says, he got his "first views of the expansion of science, and of the system of things in which we are placed." In fact, he goes as far as to avow that this good man "probably fixed the destinies of my life." For he had the happy faculty of making the road to knowledge both easy and agreeable and of infusing into his young student's mind some of his own elegance and culture and liberal spirits.

In 1762 Professor Small returned to Europe, but before then he had arranged to have Jefferson accepted as a student of law under his most intimate friend, George Wythe, who "continued to be my faithful and beloved mentor in youth, and my most affectionate friend through life."

This was a most happy circumstance, because George Wythe was one of the ablest, most sagacious, and erudite lawyers in Virginia, which prided itself on its many famous members of the bar.

Wythe was distinguished as well for his impressive manner, his sound reasoning powers, the strength of his language, often enlivened by a dash of biting cynicism. His influence on his former pupil and later colleague was a profound one. They cooperated in framing many important bills, among them the Judiciary Bill; the Chancery Bill and a bill for sequestering British property; and, above all, the Bill for Establishing Religious Freedom, in which they proclaimed *"that the opinions of men are not the object of civil government, nor under its jurisdiction."* Jefferson, though still young, was quick to defend the sanctity of men's minds.

Wythe's name will be found among the signers of the Declaration of Independence. Small and Wythe were so impressed with this youth, who was less than half their age, that they introduced him to Francis Fauquier, the governor of Virginia and one of its most distinguished citizens. The four men frequently dined together in the Governor's Palace. They formed what Jefferson called a *"partie quarrée."* These dinners always remained among his happiest memories. In 1815 he recalled:

"At these dinners I have heard more good sense, more rational and philosophical conversations, than in all my life besides. They were truly Attic societies. The Governor was musical also, and a good performer, and associated me with two or three other amateurs at his weekly concerts."

In his thoughts on female education Jefferson wrote three years later: '"Music is invaluable where a person has an ear. Where they have not, it should not be attempted. It furnishes a delightful recreation for the hours of respite from the cares of the day, and lasts us through life. The taste of this country, too, calls for this accomplishment more strongly than for either of the others [drawing or dancing]."

In music he found his supreme pleasure and peace, and this treasure he kept throughout his life, even long after he was able to play the violin.

As for dancing, he agreed that it was a necessary accomplishment for a young woman and that every affectionate parent would delight to see his daughter take part in this healthy, attractive, and elegant exercise. But he concurred with the wisdom of the "French rule . . . that no lady dances after marriage." Gestation and nursing, he believed, left "little time to a married lady when this exercise can be either safe or innocent." The innocent arts such as dancing and music and drawing not only embellish life, Jefferson believed, but furnish both amusement and happiness to those who have time on their hands.*

At thirty-five, in the flower of his manhood, he wrote to John Fabroni, his Italian music teacher:

". . . If there is a gratification, which I envy any people in this world, it is to your country its music. This is the favorite passion of my soul, and fortune has cast my lost in a country where it is in a state of deplorable barbarism."

In the same letter he told Signor Fabroni that he retained among his domestic servants a gardener, a weaver, a cabinet-maker, and a stone cutter, and that he would soon add a *vigneron*. He suggested that Fabroni might find among men who practiced these trades ones who were also proficient musicians, so that without enlarging his domestic expenses he "might have a band of two French horns, two clarinets, two hautboys, and a bassoon." He promised to meet the expenses and to make the necessary arrangements for their transportation.

For many years Jefferson practiced on his violin for three or more hours a day, and when he traveled he took with him a small violin called a kit, which he played at odd moments. Playing the fiddle was a common accomplishment among his youthful contemporaries, though how gifted a musician Jefferson was is not clear. An English captain named Bibby, with whom he played duets, considered him the best amateur whom he had ever heard; but how good a judge the captain was there is no way of knowing. Certainly Jefferson's virtuosity is of less interest to us than his enthusiastic dedication to the art. He shared his love of music with his sister Jane, who was three years his senior. There was a specially close bond between them. She was his confidante, and together they joined in their taste for the arts and much else. With

---

* For us in 20th-century America who are already facing a surfeit of leisure time, these recommendations could be taken to heart.

her melodious voice she led family singing around the fireside in the winter, or on summer evenings by the banks of the river. On these occasions, Thomas would accompany her on his violin.

Although fond of company and music and dancing and riding, he spent fourteen or fifteen hours a day at his studies. The only exercise he got was a mile run out of the city and back at twilight. He arose at dawn or as soon as he could distinguish the hands of the clock in his bedroom and retired at nine in the summer and an hour later in the winter. Extremely punctual, disciplined, meticulous, and methodical—or what today we should call "obsessional"—he was perhaps deficient in humor. But once one came to know him, one discovered his hidden warmth and loyalty and sometimes found in him a rewarding friend.

One of his closest companions was John Page, a member of the plantation aristocracy, who lived at Roswell, the largest mansion in Virginia. To him Jefferson unburdened his smitten heart. Among the young ladies he had met while at college in Williamsburg, with whom he danced in the Apollo room of the Raleigh Tavern, was Rebecca Burwell, or "Belinda," as he called her. He had fallen in love with her, or at least he was infatuated and bewitched, alternately in the clouds or in the depths of despair. On a flyleaf of one of his books he had written:

> Jane Nelson is a sweet girl,
> Betsy Page is a neat girl,
> Rebecca Burwell is the devil:
> If not the devil she's one of his imps.

He was a diffident and backward lover. In January 1763 he wrote to Page from Shadwell:

"How does R. B. do? Had I better stay here and do nothing, or go down and do less? . . . Inclination tells me to go, receive my sentence, and be no longer in suspense: but reason says, if you go, and your attempt proves unsuccessful, you will be ten times more wretched than ever." And so he wavered, tormented by doubts. Page advised his friend to talk to the girl, but Jefferson countered with: "No, no, Page; whatever assurances I may give her in private of my esteem for her . . . they must be kept in private . . . because I never can bear to remain in suspense so long a time . . . if Belinda will not accept of my service, it shall never be offered to another . . . that she will, she never gave me reason to hope."

In October of the same year he managed, in his excitement, at another dance, to blurt out a few broken phrases, but he did not propose to her. Instead, he hinted that he hoped to go abroad for a few years and also hoped that she would wait for him. His reward was the reward of the faint-hearted. Belinda soon announced that she would marry someone else. And Jefferson consoled himself by reflecting that "Perfect happiness . . . was never intended by the Deity to be the lot of one of his creatures in this world," and that "Many and great are the comforts of a single state." The affair had all the earmarks of puppy love—Jefferson was still only twenty. Although of a highly emotional nature, he managed in this and indeed throughout his life to keep a cool head, even with his heart afire.

At the end of his second year he left college, far better equipped in breadth of learning than most of his contemporaries. He combined a real love of both mathematics and the classics, thus reflecting and fulfilling the two sides of his nature—the masculine and the feminine. Mathematics was the principal passion of his life, and music—a combination frequently encountered in the great and gifted. He was a fine Latin and Greek scholar as well and read the more difficult texts with ease. These became "the most prized solaces of his old age." To a thorough knowledge of French as a written language he later added Italian and Spanish. During his law studies he mastered enough Anglo-Saxon to enable him to study the foundations of the English common law.

In metaphysics or ethics as sciences he had little interest, but he approved greatly works which fostered the moral sense, including Epictetus, Plato's *Dialogues,* and the works of Cicero, Antoninus, and Seneca. But first and foremost he placed the teachings of Christ, although Jefferson was often unjustly accused of apostasy.

He wrote to his nephew, Peter Carr, Dabney's son, that it was a waste of time to attend lectures on moral philosophy. Instead, he urged him to read good books. The writings of Sterne, for example, provided "the best course of morality that ever was written." ". . . and above all things, lose no occasion of exercising your dispositions to be grateful, to be generous, to be charitable, to be humane, to be true, just, firm, orderly, courageous, etc. Consider every act of this kind, as an exercise which will strengthen your moral faculties, and increase your worth." This list of virtues was most certainly Jefferson's very own. He was, on the whole, objective, pragmatic, and utilitarian and not given to abstractions.

In literature he placed the Greeks ahead of the Romans, Demosthenes above Cicero. His preference was also for Thucydides and Tacitus rather than for Plutarch. He had little taste for fiction beyond Sterne and Fielding and Smollett, but he did enjoy *Gil Blas* and *Don Quixote;* the latter he even read twice and with relish. When he was unable to fall asleep he would compose love and murder stories; however, he could never progress beyond three pages without dropping off.

His favorite reading included Homer and the Greek dramatists, and Horace; also Tasso, Molière, Shakespeare, Milton, Dryden, Pope, and Ossian. He was fond of copying, in his neat hand, songs by minor Italian poets and the English pastoral poets. With characteristic energy, he even studied Gaelic and Erse in order to be able to understand better Macpherson's alleged translations of Ossian, whom in his youth he regarded as the greatest poet that ever existed, an enthusiasm that appeared to cool with maturity.

Jefferson continued his law studies for the next five years, spending his summers at Shadwell with his family. During this time his sister Martha, then nineteen, married his great friend and fellow law student, Dabney Carr. Carr and Jefferson were inseparable companions. They built themselves a rustic bench under an ancient oak high up on Monticello. There they would ride out with their law books on summer mornings and pass many hours in study and congenial talk. They grew greatly attached to the spot; in fact, so much so that they made a compact: whoever of the two should die first would be buried there by the other. It was Jefferson who survived his friend by more than a half-century. True to his pact, the place became the burial ground of the Jeffersons, and to this day the two men rest on the spot where they studied together in their youth. It also became the site of his famous dwelling at Monticello.

Three months after his sister Martha and Dabney Carr were married, Jefferson's older sister, Jane, died. This, after the death of his father, was the first of many grievous losses that he was to suffer during his life. Jane's death left an ache that nothing ever quite assuaged. Even in extreme old age he often spoke of her to his grandchildren, especially after church, when the Psalm-tunes for which he always had a particular fondness brought her vividly to mind.

The April before Jane's death, Jefferson had reached his majority. He was now the head of the family, which was truncated by the marriage and departure of two of his sisters and then by the loss of Jane. He left home and hurried back to Williamsburg to resume his law studies and to be present for the opening of the General Court. It was characteristic of him to try to bury his grief by throwing himself with renewed devotion into his studies. All his life he resorted to hard work as a distraction from pain and sorrow. In this respect he was a true Puritan, with, moreover, some of the restriction and perhaps submerged anger characteristic of the Puritan. There were other important matters, as well, to occupy his mind. The famous Resolutions of 1765 against the Stamp Act were proposed by the House of Burgesses when Jefferson was still a law student. He attended the debate at the House, where, there being no visitors' gallery, he stood at the door of the lobby. The Declaratory Act, which gave the British Parliament the right to tax the American colonies, became a law in January 1765 and went into effect in November. It was in the House of Burgesses that he heard the splendid display of Patrick Henry's talents as a popular orator—talents "great indeed: such as I have never heard from any other man." All the more noteworthy to Jefferson, since Henry had lodged with him on his visits from the back woods to Williamsburg, where he had cut the figure of a coarse and crude and eccentric bumpkin. Young Jefferson was spellbound. In his *Autobiography* Jefferson speaks of Henry's "poetical fancy," and of "his sublime imagination, his lofty and overwhelming diction." William Wirt, a fellow-Virginian lawyer, was to write much later of the occasion:

"It was in the midst of this magnificent debate, while he [Henry] was descanting on the tyranny of the obnoxious act, that he exclaimed, in a voice of thunder, and with the look of a god, 'Caesar had his Brutus—Charles the First his Cromwell—and George the Third'—('Treason!' cried the Speaker—'treason! treason!' echoed from every part of the House. It was one of those trying moments which is decisive of character. Henry faltered not an instant; but rising to a loftier attitude, and fixing on the Speaker an eye of the most determined fire, he finished his sentence with the firmest emphasis)—*may profit by their example.* If *this* be treason, make the most of it!"

Jefferson's own comments on Henry are:

"Wirt says he [Henry] read Plutarch's lives once a year. I don't believe he ever read two volumes of them. On his visits to court, *he used always to put up with me.* On one occasion of the breaking up in November, to meet again in the spring, as he was departing in the morning, he looked among my books, and observed, 'Mr. J., I will take two volumes of Hume's Essays, and try to read them this winter.' On his return he brought them, saying he had not been able to get half way into one of them.

"His great delight was to put on his hunting-shirt, collect a parcel of overseers and such like people, and spend weeks together hunting in the 'piny woods,' camping at night, and cracking jokes round a light-wood fire.

"*It was to him that we were indebted for the unanimity that prevailed among us.* He would address the assemblages of the people at which he was present, in such strains of eloquence as Homer wrote in. I never heard anything that deserved to be called by the same name with what flowed from him; and where he got the torrent of language, is inconceivable.

"I have frequently shut my eyes while he spoke, and when he was done asked myself what he had said, without being able to recollect a word of it. He was no logician. He was truly a great man, however, one of enlarged views."

The ambivalence of Jefferson's feelings for Henry is fairly obvious. It hints at the fact that the two men were in most respects polar opposites both in temperament and in principle. Indeed, Jefferson's relations with Patrick Henry were one of the most troubled and enduring conflicts of his life.

CHAPTER THREE

❧ ❧

In 1769, when Jefferson was twenty-six, he was chosen a member of the House of Burgesses for Albemarle County. He was not above canvassing the county for votes, calling on each voter and pledging his vote and his influence, and often also inviting him for lunch and an unlimited supply of punch. This was accepted practice. The cakes, and the punch with which they were washed down, cost Jefferson all of forty-five shillings. When his close friend James Madison ran for office some years later without benefit of the punch bowl, he was defeated at the polls. Every voter was compelled to vote at every election, or pay for his defection with a hundred pounds of tobacco.

Jefferson stuck throughout his political career to his early resolution never to engage in any enterprise that would improve his fortune. It was a declaration of virtue that became part of his public character and won him devoted followers, even though the cynical were inclined to suspect him.

The House of Burgesses assembled on May 11, 1769, with nearly a hundred members in attendance, among them George Washington and Patrick Henry. Two years earlier, Governor Fauquier had died. And now his replacement, the Right Honorable Norborne Baron de Botetourt, had arrived, equipped by the king with a magnificent gilded state-coach drawn by six or eight milk-white horses.* The first order of business was to elect a speaker. Peyton Randolph was unanimously chosen. Then, for two days, followed an exchange of courtesies and civilities between governor and legislators. All the while the members were wholly preoccupied with resisting the taxation of the colonies by Parliament. They were greatly spirited by a dispatch from Massachusetts announcing their "firm resolve . . . to resist these duties by all constitutional means."

On the third day, five resolutions were introduced and unanimously passed, to wit: "1) No taxation without representation; 2) The colonies *may* concur and co-operate in seeking redress of grievances; 3) sending accused persons away from their country for trial is an inexpressible complexity of wrong; 4) He will send an address on these topics to the 'father of all his people, beseeching his royal interposition.' " Everyone knows the upshot of this firm stand on the part of the colonists. The governor commanded the members of the House to attend him in his council chamber. He then spoke these words: "Mr. Speaker and Gentlemen of the House of Burgesses: I have heard of your resolves, and augur ill of their effects. You have made it my duty to dissolve you, and you are dissolved accordingly."

Dissolved or not, they were undaunted. Two days later they met as private gentlemen at the Raleigh Tavern, in the same Apollo room where Jefferson had danced the minuet with his Belinda, and there they drew up and signed the non-importation agreement, following the example set by Massachusetts the year before. Every man who signed the agreement was re-elected, but every man who refused to sign failed of re-election. Lord Botetourt recognized the nature of his adversaries, knowing them to be men of honor and loyalty and in no sense rebels. He had been assured that His Majesty would lay no further tax on America and that Parliament in its next session would remove the duties on glass, paper, and colors. He gave his personal assurance that he would "exert every power with which I am or shall be legally invested, in order to obtain and maintain for the continent of America that satisfaction which I have been *authorized to prom-*

* Historical scholars are in dispute about the exact number.

ise this day, by the confidential servants of our gracious sovereign, who, to my certain knowledge, rates his honor so high, that he would rather part with his crown than preserve it by deceit."

Now that the enslavement of Virginia seemed safely bypassed, Jefferson thought the moment had come to introduce a bill giving owners a right to manumit their slaves, which the laws of Virginia then forbade. Realizing the intense feelings that such a bill would arouse, he contrived to have it introduced by a senior member, Colonel Bland; but Jefferson seconded the motion. The result of this maneuver was to have Jefferson "denounced as an enemy to his country," and "treated with the greatest indecorum." His bill was, of course, defeated, but a similar bill was voted into law thirteen years later.

The *Virginia Gazette* for September 7, 1769, printed the following advertisement:

"Run away from the subscriber in *Albemarle,* a Mulatto slave called *Sandy,* about 35 years of age, his stature is rather low, inclining to corpulence, and his complexion light; he is a shoemaker by trade, in which he uses his left hand principally, can do coarse carpenters work, and is something of a horse jockey; he is greatly addicted to drink, and when drunk is insolent and disorderly, in his conversation he swears much, and his behaviour is artful and knavish. He took with him a white horse, much scarred with traces, of which it is expected he will endeavour to dispose; he also carried his shoemakers tools, and will probably endeavour to get employment that way."

The "subscriber" to this advertisement was Thomas Jefferson, and the reward offered was from forty shillings to ten pounds, depending upon whether said slave was taken up within the county of Albemarle, elsewhere in the colony, or in any other colony.

Jefferson was now a man of property; he had inherited 1,900 acres of land. With a large household to support, including eighty-three slaves, his plantation was, however, far from profitable. The cash crops of tobacco did not yield more than two or three hundred pounds per year, and his total earnings including legal fees amounted to an annual income equivalent to about five thousand dollars. About a quarter of this sum he spent each year in purchasing books.

In his third year of legal practice he commenced the project which was to take a quarter of a century to complete; namely, building his home in Monticello. In 1769 he began to level off the top of the hill (580 feet high) on which his house was to be placed. A little one-room, red-brick building on the south end of the terrace was finished within a year. Jefferson himself planned and designed it; indeed, he was architect, builder, cabinetmaker, construction foreman, and landscape artist all in one. Almost everything needed, including nails, was made on the plantation.

The dwelling was finished just in time. Shortly after he moved in, the house at Shadwell, where Jefferson had been born, and where his mother and her unmarried children still lived, burned to the ground. They found temporary, cramped quarters in the overseer's house. All Jefferson's books, papers, and records were destroyed. His books alone, according to a letter he wrote his friend Page, were valued at two hundred pounds sterling. When Jefferson asked the slave who brought him the news of the fire about his books, he was told that they were all burned, but that his fiddle had been saved. Within three years, however, he had accumulated a new library which, exclusive of the volumes of music and the books he kept in Williamsburg, amounted to more than 1,200 volumes.

He was not a man who could live without books, nor, for that matter, without growing things. His account-book for 1771 shows that he was busy making plans for his future residence. Of the grounds, he wrote in his orderly way:

"Thin the trees. Cut out stumps and undergrowth. Remove old trees and other rubbish, except where they may look well. Cover the whole with grass. Intersperse jessamine, honeysuckle, sweetbrier, and even hardy flowers which may not require attention. Keep in it deer, rabbits, peacocks, guinea poultry, pigeons, etc. Let it be an asylum for hares, squirrels, pheasants, partridges, and every other wild animal (except those of prey). Court them to it, by laying food for them in proper places. Procure a buck-elk, to be, as it were, monarch of the wood; but keep him shy, that his appearance may not lose its effect by too much familiarity."

Among the shrubs, he listed alder, bastard indigo, barberry, cleanthus, clethra, laurel, sweetbrier; among trees, lilac, wild cherry, dogwood, red bud, horse chestnut, catalpa, magnolia, mulberry, and locust; and for evergreens, holly, juniper, and yew; and also a great variety of hardy perennials.

These practical specifications were preceded by written jottings and musings both sentimental and romantic about a burying place, a spring, and a grotto. Even an inscription in pentameter was provided for:

"Nymph of the grot, these sacred springs I keep,
And to the murmur of these waters sleep;
Ah! Spare my slumbers! gently tread the cave!
And drink in silence, or in silence lave!"

Jefferson's home-building was the natural precursor to his marriage. He had previously jotted down, perhaps for his own satisfaction, the specifications for the perfect wife. Sweetness of temper, affection to a husband, and attention to his interests were the basis of matrimonial felicity, he thought. "Never consider as a trifle what may please him." Indeed, to please that one person should be "a thought never absent from your conduct." He admitted that wedlock even at its happiest is not exempted from the common fate of all sublunary blessings. The office of a wife includes the exertion of a friend. There were situations in which to love, to cherish, and to obey would not be enough; a wife must teach her husband to be at peace with himself and to be reconciled to the world.

These were the musings of a celibate, perhaps one just on the brink of falling in love. He had a good example in his dear friend Dabney Carr, whose happiness in his marriage to Jefferson's sister in 1765 was obvious to all. Jefferson was now seriously moved by the young widow of Bathurst Skelton, a student whom he had known at William and Mary. This was no mere infatuation as with his Belinda. Martha Skelton was the daughter of John Wayles of Lancashire, whose plantation was known as The Forest. Wayles was a practicing lawyer in Williamsburg and also an enterprising slave-trader who had amassed a handsome fortune. His daughter Martha had married at seventeen, but her husband, Bathurst Skelton, died after two years of marriage, leaving her with an infant son. This child survived until after Mrs. Skelton married Thomas Jefferson four years later.

It is not known when Jefferson first met Martha Wayles—whether before her first marriage or during it. In early October 1770 he called on her, and again on December tenth and on the twentieth for the Christmas holidays. During 1771 his visits to The Forest increased; he was there every ten days or fortnight. By June he had ordered a fortepiano for her, in place of the clavichord he had intended. He specified that "the case be of fine mahogany, solid not veneered, the compass from Double G to F in alt, a plenty of spare strings; and the workmanship of the whole very handsome and worthy of a lady for whom I intend it."

In August 1771 Jefferson was begging his friend Robert Skipworth to "offer prayers for me too at that shrine to which tho' absent I pray continual devotions. In every scheme of happiness she is placed in the foreground of the picture, as the principal figure. Take that away and it is no picture for me."

One of his friends, an older woman, Mrs. Drummond, was cheering him on from the sidelines. She said to him, ". . . persevere thou, good young man, persevere. She has good sense . . . and I hope will not refuse (the blessing, shall I say)—why not, as I think it—of your hand. . . . I most sincerely wish you the full completion of all your wishes, both as to the lady and everything else."

What delayed Jefferson in his courtship we do not know: perhaps a certain diffidence that was always apparent in him. Perhaps he was still tied to his mother and could not easily take another woman for a wife. It is no accident, of course, that the woman he did marry was a widow with an infant son. This probably made it seem a less hazardous venture and also gratified, in a way surely hidden from him, his longings for maternal love.

They were married on New Year's Day in 1772 at The Forest in Charles City County, where the bride's father, John Wayles, lived. She was twenty-three; her husband, thirty.

Their license-bond for marriage was written in Jefferson's own clear, frank, and pleasing hand. The word "spinster" was stricken out, but can still be read; it was replaced by "widow," apparently inserted in another handwriting, though some think it was probably Jefferson's.

Martha was described as beautiful, with large, expressive hazel eyes and luxuriant auburn hair, a little above middle height, with a lithe and exquisitely formed figure, a model of graceful and queenlike carriage. She was well-educated for her day, a constant reader, meticulous in keeping her accounts. In addition to all these virtues, she had a well-cultivated talent for music. "She walked, rode, and danced, with admirable grace and spirit—sung, and played the spinet and harpsichord . . . with uncommon skill." She "possessed excellent sense and a lively play of fancy; and had a frank, warm-hearted, and somewhat impulsive disposition." In truth, the bride and groom seem to have been made for each other. They were matched in tastes and habits, in love of music, gaiety, even somewhat in the color of their hair. They had the congenial interests which, of all the ingredients of a good marriage, seem to head the list.

In a light snowfall, the pair left The Forest bound for Monticello, a hundred miles distant, traveling at first in a carriage, which they had to abandon, however, when the depth of the snow exceeded two feet. They then proceeded on horseback along a mountain track, leaving Colonel Carter's estate, Blenheim, at sundown, with Monticello still eight miles away.* When they arrived, it was late at night, the fires were out, and the servants had all retired to their own houses. One can imagine the chill dreariness of the reception afforded by the little pavilion, which was the only part of the house then habitable. But they soon warmed the scene with their own gaiety and love and merriment and song, and with part of a bottle of wine hidden on a shelf behind some books. Anyone who has ever been snowed in knows the special kind of delight this can bring if there is food enough and a warm fire burning in the hearth, and, above all, a congenial companion.

By January 25, according to Jefferson's garden book, the snow

* Or, according to Jefferson's "table of distances," 8.01 miles!

lay three feet deep, the deepest ever seen in Albemarle County, which spread out at their feet, below the mountaintop. From there they could see the Rivanna River and half a mile beyond it the blackened ruin of Shadwell. The village of Charlottesville with its surrounding farms and the river winding among them lay in the foreground. In the middle distance they could see a solitary pyramidal peak, and beyond it, a hundred miles distant against the horizon, the Blue Ridge. All in all, an ideal spot for a honeymoon. They entertained themselves by reading Ossian's poems together. Jefferson had found that the so-called Macpherson's version was but a poor translation of the poems from the Gaelic. However, of these poems he said that "the glow of one warm thought is to me worth more than money."

There was at this moment a lull in the political storm. With the exception of two absences in April and October to attend the General Court in Williamsburg, Jefferson spent most of the year on his mountain, leveling the summit to an expanse of six acres; cutting roads and paths through the woods; and constantly observing, recording, and experimenting. He even matched the efficiency and carrying capacity of a one-wheeled barrow against a two-wheeled one, and he counted the number of rails or cords of wood that could be drawn up the mountain by a four-horse wagon. He found that a coach and six could turn in eighty feet, and he allowed enough room for high-born visitors arriving in such vehicles, though he himself rode in nothing grander than a two-wheeled chaise. His grounds were enclosed by a fence with alternating long and short pickets. He allowed four nails to the short picket and five to the long. In all his domestic arrangements there is evidence of this precision.

In his garden he constantly experimented, trying a great variety of trees, shrubs, grasses, grains, vegetables, bulbs, fruits and nuts, including chestnuts from France, Alpine strawberries, melons and grapes from Italy. He was greatly assisted by his neighbor Philip Mazzei, who had started a vineyard nearby and furnished Jefferson with some experienced Italian gardeners.

By March 20, Jefferson had sowed a patch of late peas; by July fifteen cucumbers came to his table, and he planted out celery, a patch of peas for the fall, and snap beans; on July 31 he had Irish potatoes from the garden. On October 8 he gathered two plumb-peaches at Monticello. A few weeks before this, his first-born, Martha Jefferson, had arrived, she who was to contribute so much to the solace of her father's life. He was now more than ever bound to his estate and to his beautiful, delicate, companionable, and helpful wife.

CHAPTER FOUR

❦

A little more than a year after their marriage Martha Jefferson's father, John Wayles, died. He left her one-third of his fortune, or forty thousand acres of land and 135 slaves, including a whole family of "bright mulattoes" who were known to be close kin to Martha, being her own father's children by a slave mother. (Jefferson's political enemies naturally made the most of this situation and accused him of fathering a whole brood of slaves by Sally Hemings, or "Black Sal," the handsomest woman in this mulatto family.) The portion which came to Martha Jefferson after the debts on the estate were paid by her husband amounted to a sum about equal to the value of Jefferson's own property. This debt of £3,749 12s. he assumed, and in order to pay it off he had to sell some of his land. Payments in paper were made to the Loan Office, but the value of paper depreciated so precipitously that Jefferson was forced to sell property again both in 1787 and in 1792. These additional payments swept away nearly half his estate.

Although he was often charged with extravagance and with having a poor business head, there is little evidence for these charges. Actually, he managed to double his estate before he was thirty years old, and had it not been for the British debts which came to him from his late father-in-law, Jefferson could be described as affluent. He acquired Poplar Forest, in Bedford County, which remained one of his favorite retreats, serving as an occasional residence up to the time of his death. But he lived modestly in a house no bigger than a porter's lodge, and the phaeton he drove cut no great figure. His only expensive taste was for fine horses—a taste which lasted throughout his life. His preference was for Virginia thoroughbreds, and he seldom rode or was willing to drive any other than these. He usually kept half a dozen brood-mares in his stables, until Lord Cornwallis arrived and made off with them, killing their foals at the same time.

With other Virginia gentlemen he enjoyed horse racing, although he never ran but a single race himself. He was described as a bold and fearless rider, with an easy and confident seat. He showed impatience and temper only when his mount proved stubborn or restive. Then he used both whip and spurs. Contrary to custom in Virginia, Jefferson rode out alone; he did not like being followed by a servant. He rarely drew rein for broken ground and thought nothing of dashing through the Rivanna, even when the stream was flooded and swollen. Something of his romantic nature can be gleaned from the names he gave his superb chargers: Cucullin, The General, Wildair, Caractacus, Tarquin, Diomed, Arcturus, Jacobin, Celer, and Eagle. Eagle was the last of this fiery string. In his old age, when Jefferson was so feeble that he had to be helped into his saddle, a messenger arrived from Charlottesville late one evening announcing that Jefferson's grandson had met with a serious accident. Although night was settling in, Jefferson immediately had Eagle brought to the door. Against the entreaties of his family, he was helped into the saddle, and he struck the spirited animal such a blow that it bounded forward at a full gallop, clattering through the notch and racing down the rough and steep descent into Charlottesville in record time.

But when he was still only twenty-nine, strong and wiry, he could easily jump into his saddle. His garden book gives some notion of his activities and interests. He had the habit of marking many entries with asterisks, and these he would later transcribe into their appropriate places in other notebooks. For example:

"In making a stone wall in my garden, I find by an accurate

calculation that 7½ cubical feet may be done in a day by one hand, who brings his own stone into place and does everything."

"Mrs. Wythe puts one-tenth very rich superfine Malmesey to a dry Madeira, and makes a fine wine."

Among the articles for contracts with overseers are to be found the following items:

"Allow one-half share [of grain] for every horse, and the same for ploughboy. . . . Provision 400 lb. pork if single; 500 lb., if married. And never to bleed a negro."

The time was rapidly approaching when he could no longer supervise the work on his estates and when most of it had to be left to overseers—many of them, to his own detriment, shiftless, if not dishonest. Between 1772 and 1782 his increasing part in public affairs kept him from home much of the time, although he insisted that he wanted more than anything to be at home with his family, with his flowers and fruit trees, and his agricultural experiments and pursuits.

During this decade his wife gave birth to six children—all daughters but one. Of the six, only two, Martha and Mary, lived beyond infancy. There is scant mention of this source of grief to him. He was not given to displaying his intimate feelings in public; in fact, he took special pains to conceal them. This has raised the question from some as to whether, indeed, he had deep feelings. There seems little doubt that he did, but he kept a firm check on them and seldom allowed himself to give them free rein. Since he was always ready to resort to his pen, as was his wife, it is remarkable that among his voluminous letters nothing remains of the correspondence that must have passed between them during his long absences. In his published letters, he mentions her only about a half-dozen times, and then usually to speak of his concern over her persistent ill-health.

A few months after the birth of their first child events occurred —not, to be sure, in Virginia, but in Rhode Island and Massachusetts—which forced Jefferson into public life.

These were the affair in Narragansett Bay, when the British gun boat *Gaspée* was set afire by the men of Providence; and the closing of the port of Boston after the famous Tea Party. Both of

these episodes excited passionate interest and sympathy throughout the colonies—perhaps especially in Virginia, always closely
tied to Massachusetts in its sense of independence and love of liberty.

After the *Gaspée* incident, Parliament retaliated by passing an
act making any destruction of His Majesty's property punishable
by death. Virginia quickly came to the defense of little Rhode Island, so different from herself in wealth, in power, in political
tradition, ideals, and loyalties. The time had come to set aside
these differences and to unite in resistance to the crown. Accordingly, a committee was organized in the House of Burgesses in
March 1773, known as a Committee of Correspondence, to serve
as "the best instrument for intercommunication" among the colonies.

This committee was required to draw up and propose resolutions and also to arrange a meeting of deputies from every colony
at some central place, in order to obtain the earliest and most au-
thentic intelligence of all proceedings in England in regard to the
colonies. Thomas Jefferson was named by the consulting members to move the resolutions. But he urged that this should be
done not by himself but by Dabney Carr, his friend and brother-
in-law, then a new member. Jefferson believed that the members
should be given the opportunity to hear Carr and should be made
aware of his many talents and exceptional worth. Carr did move
the resolutions, to great effect, on the twelfth of March, in a
speech remarkable for its force and eloquence. He was supported
in his motion by Patrick Henry and Richard Henry Lee. The
motion passed without dissent.

Governor Dunmore, who had succeeded Lord Botetourt the
previous year, immediately dissolved the House. Jefferson realized that the most urgent of all measures was that of coming to an
understanding with all the other colonies, in order to consider
the British claims as a common cause to all and to produce unity
of action. He was therefore one of the earliest sponsors of the
Committee of Correspondence and was now actively launched on
his political career. But he was mistaken in believing that Virginia had the honor of being the first to institute such a commit-

tee. Three years earlier, the Massachusetts assembly, under the in-
stigation of John Adams, had appointed a committee for the same
purpose, but it does not appear to have acted.

Carr's appearance before the House of Burgesses moved
Thomas Jefferson to say:

"I well remember the pleasure expressed in the countenance
and conversation of the members generally, on this début of Mr.
Carr, and the hopes they conceived as well from the talents as the
patriotism it manifested. . . . His character was of a high order. A
spotless integrity, sound judgment, handsome imagination, en-
riched by education and reading, quick and clear in his concep-
tions, of correct and ready elocution, impressing every hearer
with the sincerity of the heart from which it flowed. His firmness
was inflexible in whatever he thought was right; but when no
moral principle stood in the way, never had man more of the
milk of human kindness, of indulgence, of softness, of pleasantry
of conversation and conduct. The number of his friends, and the
warmth of their affection, were proofs of his worth, and of their
estimate of it."

This exceptionally gifted young man had made his first and last
speech before the House of Burgesses in mid-April of 1773, when
he was twenty-nine years old. Thirty-five days later he was dead.
He had succumbed to an acute and violent attack of bilious fever
(typhoid) in Charlottesville and was too sick to be moved home
to Shadwell, where later he was buried. But Jefferson, true to his
youthful pledge, directed that his body be disinterred and moved
to a grave beneath their favorite oak at Monticello. On the grave
Jefferson had inscribed: "To his Virtue, Good Sense, Learning,
and Friendship this stone is dedicated by Thomas Jefferson, who,
of all men living, loved him most."

Carr's poor widow, ill from a recent confinement, was overwhelmed and submerged in despairing grief, but her brother, as
one would expect of him, took Martha Carr and her six children
into his own house, where he brought them up and educated
them as his own children.

The death of Dabney Carr was a grievous loss to Jefferson, but
he had little time to spare for his emotions. Within a year public

events commanded his best energies, and he had to turn away from domesticity. With the closing of the port of Boston, Jefferson and a few like-minded associates in the Virginia assembly, including, among others, Patrick Henry, Richard Henry Lee, and his brother Francis Lightfoot Lee, agreed that they "must boldly take an unequivocal stand in the line with Massachusetts. . . ." They were convinced that what the people needed was to be aroused from their lethargy, and to that end they proposed a day of general fasting, humiliation, and prayer. They selected the first day of June for this purpose, since it was the day on which the Port Bill was to take effect. By their devotions they hoped not only to avert the evils of civil war but also "to turn the hearts of the King and Parliament to moderation and justice." The House approved the measure without opposition, but the next day, as might have been predicted, Governor Dunmore applied the accustomed remedy and again dissolved it. Then the members resorted to their usual device. They assembled in the Apollo room, entered into an association, and denounced wholeheartedly England's high-handed policy and behavior. An attack on one colony they considered an attack on all, and they recommended the holding of a general annual congress. Mr. Jefferson said that the effect of the day was electric. He and John Walker were chosen from Albemarle County as deputies to the convention. Albemarle alone among twenty-nine Virginia counties declared that the colonies were wholly independent of Parliament, and were free to enact their own laws and subject to no others. These had been Jefferson's views from the beginning of the colony's differences with Britain, but he had been able to get no one to agree with him except Mr. Wythe.

On August 1, in Williamsburg, the Virginia Convention was to meet to appoint delegates to represent the colony in the general congress. On his way to the Convention, Jefferson was seized with a violent attack of dysentery which prevented him from attending. He did, however, prepare instructions for the direction of the delegates. These were printed in pamphlet form under the title "A Summary View of the Rights of British America," widely read and approved by the members of the convention, although others, including Patrick Henry, found it too bold for the present state of things. Actually, the "Summary View" was "a declaration of independence nearly two years in advance of the adopted one." It is the more remarkable when we consider that it was the work of a young man of thirty-one who held no office, other than that of burgess, was in no way a firebrand, and was outdistanced in power and public distinction by such men as John Hancock, the Adamses, Patrick Henry, and Peyton Randolph.

A few passages from the peroration of this document must be reproduced here, if only to make heard the orchestration of Jefferson's noble prose:

"That these are our grievances, which we have thus laid before his Majesty, with that freedom of language and sentiment which becomes a free people, *claiming their rights as derived from the laws of nature, and not as the gift of their chief magistrate.* Let those flatter, who fear; it is not an American art. To give praise where it is not due might be well from the venal, but would ill beseem those who are asserting the rights of human nature. They know, and will, therefore, say, that Kings *are the servants, not the proprietors of the people.* Open your breast, Sire, to liberal and expanded thought. Let not the name of George the Third be a blot on the page of history. . . . The whole art of government consists in the art of being honest. Only aim to do your duty, and mankind will give you credit where you fail. . . . *The God who gave us life, gave us liberty,* at the same time: the hand of force may destroy, but cannot disjoin them. This, Sire, is our last, our determined resolution."

When the second Convention of Virginia met in Richmond in March of 1775, Jefferson was one of the representatives of Albemarle. He undoubtedly heard Patrick Henry's words, which have thundered down the ages ever since they were spoken. The scene was described by an old Baptist clergyman who was present:

"Henry rose with an unearthly fire burning in his eyes. He commenced somewhat calmly—but the smothered excitement began more and more to play upon his features and thrill in the tones of his voice. The tendons of his neck stood out white and rigid 'like whipcords.' His voice rose louder and louder, until the walls of the building, and all within them, seemed to shake and reek in its tremendous vibrations. Finally, his pale face and glaring eye became 'terrible to look upon.' Men 'leaned forward in their seats,' with their heads 'strained forward,' their faces pale, and their eyes glaring like the speaker's. His last exclamation—'Give me liberty or give me death'—was like the shout of the leader which turns back the rout of battle!"

These famous words were spoken on the twenty-third of March 1775. Patrick Henry carried the Convention with him. It was agreed that the people must arm.

On the eleventh of June, Jefferson took his seat in the Continental Congress at Philadelphia. It required ten days to travel from Monticello by phaeton with two spare horses, stopping on the way at King William Court House, Fredericksburg, Port Tobacco, Upper Marlborough, Annapolis, Rockhall, and Wilmington. The traveler made careful note of the differences in rates of exchange as he crossed each colonial border—another example of his inveterate precision. It was like him to pursue his pedantic recordings, in spite of the momentous events in which he was soon to be embroiled.

When he arrived in Philadelphia, Congress had already been sitting for six weeks. His reputation as the author of "A Summary View . . ." had gone before him, and he came armed with Virginia's answer, which he himself had written, to Lord North's "Conciliatory Proposition." Despite his youth, because of his great gifts of expression, he was chosen to succeed Peyton Randolph as the president of Congress, where he was received with rousing enthusiasm by his fellow members.

John Adams said of him later:

"Mr. Jefferson came into Congress in June, 1775, and brought a reputation for literature, science, and a happy talent of composition. Writings of his were handed about remarkable for the peculiar felicity of expression." He was already known for his masterly pen, because of the public paper he had written for the House of Burgesses.

In a letter to Timothy Pickering, Adams wrote of Jefferson: "Though a silent member in Congress, he was so prompt, frank, explicit, and decisive upon committees and in conversation—*not even Samuel Adams was more so*—that he soon seized upon my heart."

Adams was more impetuous, impulsive, partisan, and prejudiced, but the two men appealed to each other in spite of the differences that later split them apart for a time.

Five days after taking his seat in Congress, Jefferson was appointed along with John Dickinson to a committee charged with drawing up a declaration of the cause for taking up arms. The committee had already rendered its report, but Congress had not approved it. Now with the addition of Jefferson and Dickinson (who still clung to his conservative views and to the hope of reconciliation with Britain), a new report was submitted and accepted. Jefferson accomplished this without altercation or quarreling and without arrogating to himself any exceptional merit or credit. He early displayed his great talent for getting things done without creating ill-will. He was as resolute as he had been in the Virginia House of Burgesses not to allow a schism to divide the members, no matter how extreme or divergent their views, but always to keep the front and the rear together; he remained conspicuously free from vanity and false pride, often giving credit to others for his own accomplishments.

In preparing this new address, Dickinson saved the last four and a half paragraphs from Jefferson's original draft, and to these it owed most of its popularity and its thundering reception. But not until he was seventy-seven did Jefferson make any mention of his own share in its preparation.

This report "on the Causes of taking up Arms" was presented to the Congress on July 6.

The first lines of the peroration are pure Jefferson:

"We are reduced to the alternative of choosing an unconditional submission to the tyranny of irritable ministers, or resistance by force. The latter is our choice. We have counted the cost of this contest, and find nothing so dreadful as voluntary slavery. . . . Our cause is just. Our union is perfect—our internal resources are great. . . . Against violence actually offered, we have taken up arms. We shall lay them down when hostilities shall cease on the part of the aggressors, and all danger of their being renewed shall be removed, and not before."

On July 22, Congress chose by ballot a committee to consider Lord North's "Conciliatory Proposition." Those elected were Franklin, Jefferson, John Adams, and Richard Henry Lee, with Jefferson designated by his colleagues to draft the paper. This constituted the final solemn rejection of the British ultimatum. Congress adjourned after acting on this on the first of August. Jefferson was, to the last, reluctant to take the inevitable step of separating from the mother country. In his reluctance he was joined by such men as John Jay, the Adamses, and Benjamin Franklin, perhaps the most seasoned and the wisest of them all. Indeed, at the time, Jefferson stated that "a separation from Great Britain, and establishment of Republican Government, had never yet entered into any person's mind."

As late as November 20, 1775, he wrote to Peyton Randolph's brother, John, who had quit Virginia to return to England: "Believe me, my dear sir, there is not in the British empire, a man who more cordially loves a union with Great Britain, than I do." Just a few months before, he had written to the same gentleman: "My first wish is a restoration of our just rights; my second, a return of the happy period, when, consistently with duty, I may withdraw myself totally from the public stage, and pass the rest of my days in domestic ease and tranquillity, banishing every desire of ever hearing what passes in the world."

This was to become the familiar and recurrent theme of Jefferson's life, a constant reiteration of his major conflict between doing his grim duty and returning to domestic peace and tranquillity, far from the madding crowd.

CHAPTER FIVE

❧ ❦

During the summer and autumn of 1775 Jefferson busied himself by making additions to his house, improving the grounds and roads, and extending his kitchen garden with specimens collected from all over the country and even from abroad. His household now numbered 117, of whom thirty-four were free and eighty-three were slaves. His daughter Martha was nearly three; Jane Randolph, his second child, died in September, at eighteen months. Within six months his mother died, but there is only a brief, matter-of-fact notation of this event in his pocket account-book. It seems to have been almost impossible for him to give outward expression to his private emotions. These events and some others prevented him from taking his seat in Congress until May 14, 1776, although Congress had been almost continually in session during the elapsed year.

England's policy and behavior continued to be warlike in the extreme. Confiscation of American vessels and cargoes, impressment of American crews into the Royal Navy, were authorized and practiced. The warnings of Chatham and Fox and Burke did not stay events, made more odious by the arrival of German mercenaries, who came, it was said, as reluctantly as the British troops had come.

The day after Jefferson resumed his seat (May 15), Congress adopted a resolution with a preamble written by John Adams, in whose mind the events of Lexington and Concord had left little doubt as to the necessary course of action. This resolution was in itself a bold step toward independence, for which the way had been cleared by the publication, four months earlier, of Thomas Paine's *Common Sense*.

Up to the time Jefferson had left his home for Philadelphia, he had played an active part in the Virginia Convention; and, besides, he had been collecting money by voluntary subscription to buy powder to be used in Virginia and for the relief of the city of Boston. This activity as well as his wife's illness probably accounted for his late arrival. Whatever the cause of his delay, he was almost immediately placed on the committee charged with drafting the Declaration of Independence.

But there was further delay. Of this, Jefferson wrote in his eminently reasonable but picturesque style:

"It appearing in the course of these debates, that the Colonies of New York, New Jersey, Pennsylvania, Delaware, Maryland, and South Carolina were not yet matured for falling from the parent stem, but that they were fast advancing to that state it was thought most prudent to wait a while for them, and to postpone the final decision to July 1st. . . ."

On June 11 Congress chose by ballot the committee to prepare the Declaration. It consisted of five members in the following order: Thomas Jefferson, John Adams, Benjamin Franklin, Roger Sherman, and Robert R. Livingston. Richard Henry Lee, the mover of the resolution, was not among them; because of his wife's illness he had to leave Philadelphia hurriedly on the day the committee was appointed. He was, however, named to another committee for preparing the Articles of Confederation and, according to John Adams, ". . . it was not thought convenient that the same person should be upon both."

John Adams, commenting on Jefferson's appointment as chairman of this committee, had this to say:

"Mr. Jefferson had been now about a year a member of Congress, but had attended his duty in the House a very small part of the time, and, when there, had never spoken in public. During the whole time I sat with him in Congress, I never heard him utter three sentences together. It will naturally be inquired how it happened that he was appointed on a committee of such importance. There were more reasons than one. Mr. Jefferson had the reputation of a masterly pen; he had been chosen a delegate in Virginia, in consequence of a very handsome public paper he had written for the House of Burgesses, which had given him the character of a fine writer. *Another reason was that Mr. Richard Henry Lee was not beloved by most of his colleagues from Virginia and Mr. Jefferson was set up to rival and supplant him.* This could be done only by the pen, for Mr. Jefferson could stand no competition with him or any one else in elocution and public debate."

It is no uncommon observation that men who are shy and relatively tongue-tied can express their ideas clearly in writing.

At another point Adams wrote:

"Jefferson was chairman because he had most votes; and he had most votes *because we united in him to the exclusion of R. H. Lee, and to keep out Harrison.*"

To be sure, the above passages were written at a time when Adams was estranged from Jefferson, before the friendly offices of Dr. Benjamin Rush brought the two men together again. In addition, it is just conceivable that Adams may have been a little piqued, because Jefferson received one more vote than he did. But he himself voted for Jefferson, and it is certain that he held him in high regard. Politics, log-rolling, and intrigue in the United States are obviously no new inventions. There was plenty of each in the Continental Congress.

Among some of these master politicians there were both suspicion and hostility toward General Washington; in John Adams it was ill-concealed. But Jefferson was always Washington's loyal friend. He was simply not given to irritability and backbiting, nor did he allow himself to be drawn into the senseless battles which the Lees waged both with John Jay and with Benjamin Franklin. He had no taste for cliques and cabals, nor for intrigues and imbroglios, although he was just as intrepid a fighter for independence as were the other revolutionary stalwarts.

Jefferson was unanimously pressed to prepare the draft for the

Declaration of Independence. This he did with what has been called "that felicitous, haunting cadence which is the peculiar quality of Jefferson's best writing." Before submitting it to the full committee he showed it to Dr. Franklin and John Adams, for their comments and corrections. They made only a few simple word changes. It was then laid before the whole committee, and on the twenty-eighth of June he presented it to Congress, where it was immediately read and tabled. On July 2 the house, sitting as a committee of the whole, took Jefferson's draft from the table and proceeded to debate its adoption during the two succeeding days.

Jefferson wrote about this debate in his memoir:

"The pusillanimous idea that we had friends in England worth keeping terms with, still haunted the minds of many. For this reason, those passages which conveyed censure on the people of England were struck out, lest they should give them offence. The clause, too, reprobating the enslaving the inhabitants of Africa, was struck out in complaisance to South Carolina and Georgia, who had never attempted to restrain the importation of slaves, and who, on the contrary, still wished to continue it. Our northern brethren also, I believe, felt a little tender under the censures; for though their people had very few slaves themselves, yet they had been pretty considerable carriers of them to others."

On the evening of July 4 the Declaration as amended in committee was reported to the House and signed by every member present except Dickinson. The delegates from New York did not sign until July 15, and from Pennsylvania not until five days after that. Among these late signers was Dr. Benjamin Rush.

Nearly a half-century after the signing, Jefferson wrote in a letter to Dr. John Mease (September 26, 1825):

"At the time of writing that instrument, I lodged in the house of a Mr. Graaf, a new brick house, three stories high, of which I rented the second floor, consisting of a parlor and bed-room ready furnished. In that parlor I wrote habitually, and in it wrote this paper, particularly. So far I state from written proofs in my possession."

From here Jefferson trusted to memory. He thought that Mr.

Graaf had been a bricklayer and that his house was on the south side of Market Street. He had some idea that it was a corner house. His account-book shows that he took lodgings there on May 23 and that his weekly rent was thirty-five shillings sterling. He ate most of his meals at the City Tavern.

The small desk on which he wrote the Declaration of Independence he designed himself. It was made by Jefferson's Negro head-carpenter and joiner. Unfortunately, it was later lost at sea on the way from Richmond to Boston, where it was being sent to Jefferson's granddaughter Ellen, who had married Joseph Coolidge, Jr. Later, Jefferson had a replica of it made and sent to Mr. Coolidge.

The Declaration did not pass Congress without meeting impassioned resistance, which Jefferson himself likened, in a letter to Madison, to "the ceaseless action of gravity weighing upon us by night and by day." But he said not a word for it himself, thinking it "a duty to be, on that occasion, a passive auditor of the opinions of others, more impartial judges than I could be, of its merits or demerits." Dr. Franklin observed that the author of the Declaration was "writhing a little under the acrimonious criticism"; or, as Jefferson elsewhere put it, "I was sitting by Dr. Franklin, who perceived that I was not insensible to these mutilations." Franklin told him that he had made it a rule to avoid becoming the draftsman of papers to be reviewed by a public body.

John Adams rose to the occasion and became the champion of the Declaration on the floor of Congress, defending with heroic and fearless passion every word of the document. He fought like the parents of an abused or threatened child. Jefferson acknowledged his indebtedness to Adams many times, calling him "the colossus in that debate." No matter what the future held for these two men by way of temporary chill and alienation, Jefferson never begrudged the grand old man his due credit and praise. He gave great credit also to Samuel Adams, the man of the Revolution, calling him "truly a great man, wise in counsel, fertile in resources, immovable in his purposes. . . ."

In drafting the Declaration, Jefferson was charged with lack of originality. Adams himself wrote Timothy Pickering, "There is not an idea in it but what had been hackneyed in Congress for two years before." To this, Richard Henry Lee added his grain of spite, accusing Jefferson of having copied the draft from Locke's treatise on government. But Jefferson countered with this statement: "I know only that I turned to neither book nor pamphlet while writing it. I did not consider it as any part of my charge to invent new ideas altogether and to offer no sentiment which had ever been expressed before."

The essential thing was "Not to find out new principles, or new arguments, never before thought of, not merely to say things which had never been said before; but to place before mankind the common sense of the subject, in terms so plain and firm as to command their assent. . . . Neither aiming at originality of principles or sentiments, nor yet copied from any particular and previous writing, it was intended to be an expression of the American mind. . . . All its authority rests then on the harmonizing sentiments of the day, whether expressed in conversation, in letters, printed essays, in the elementary books of public right, as Aristotle, Cicero, Locke, Sidney, etc."

In its form and phraseology the Declaration "follows closely certain sentences in Locke's second treatise on government," with which most Americans were familiar "as a kind of political gospel."

Jefferson knew this. He was remarkably free from false pride or personal vainglory, and he was ready to pledge his life, his fortune, and his sacred honor for what he believed true.

During the three days of this bitter debate, Jefferson continued his cool, humorless, and accustomed entries in his pocket notebook. On July 1, 1776, the temperature was 81½ degrees at nine A.M.; on July 4 it was 68 degrees at six A.M., 78½ degrees at nine P.M. On July 1, Jefferson paid eight pence for ferrying his horses. On the third, he gave Dr. Gilmer seven shillings sixpence "for myself." On the fourth of July, he paid one Sparhawk eight pounds and fifteen shillings for a thermometer, twenty-seven shillings for 7 pairs of women's gloves, and having thus indulged himself, he chalked up one shilling and sixpence to charity.

Thursday, July 4, 1776, was hot, as a Philadelphia summer day can be. The assembled delegates were sweating not only because of the temperature and humidity but from the tension and excitement in the air. Under these circumstances, jokes, even macabre ones, serve to clear the atmosphere like a clap of thunder. There were many such. Perhaps the most famous was the exchange between John Hancock and Benjamin Franklin. When Hancock urged the necessity of all hanging together, Franklin countered with: "Yes, we must indeed all hang together, or else, most assuredly, we shall all hang separately."

But worse than the heat and the excitement were the flies. Near the hall where the debates were held was a livery stable from which swarms of flies emerged to enter through the open windows. Stable flies resemble house flies, but for their nasty bite. The honorable members, in their silk stockings, lashed the flies furiously with their handkerchiefs, but to no avail. In his old age, Jefferson recalled this scene with great merriment. In fact, he always believed that it was due to this extreme annoyance that the members signed the document so readily and brought the momentous occasion to a close.

The draft was received with rapture. It assured its author everlasting fame. On Monday, July 8, at noon, it was publicly read for the first time in Independence Square from a platform which had been erected by Rittenhouse for observing the transit of Venus. In New York, on Bowling Green, the leaden statue of George III rolled in the dust and was cast into bullets. Virginia struck George's name from the prayer book, and even little Rhode Island made it a misdemeanor, punishable by a fine of a hundred thousand pounds, to pray for the king *as* king.

Before Congress adjourned on that memorable day, Dr. Franklin, Adams, and Jefferson were appointed to a committee to devise a seal for the United States of America. *E pluribus unum* was the result of their deliberations.

Having accomplished this, Jefferson asked to be released from his seat in Congress. Twice he had been refused, but now, because of his wife's illness and his pressing duties in his native state, where he had been elected to his old seat in the legislature, his release was granted. He left Philadelphia for home in September.

Jefferson now found himself in an acute conflict between his public duty and the demands of his private life, especially in his ties to wife and home—a recurring conflict throughout his life. Seen subjectively, this was the clash between his dependent needs and his independent self-assertiveness. The conflict could not resolve itself and culminated finally in Jefferson's withdrawing from Congress and returning to the care of his sick wife. It is probable that he would have withdrawn in any case, and that this episode represented only one of many constantly repeating rationalizations in his life—alternations or oscillations between the masculine and feminine sides of this complicated man.

This conflict in itself is not unusual. But in Jefferson's case it was conspicuous because of the rapid alternations. As soon as one side found outward expression, its opposite demanded a hearing. His strength was deeply impaired by these oscillations. But he managed to borrow strength by associating himself with strong men. One can trace this tendency to his adolescence, when Thomas lost his strong, self-reliant, and wholly dependable father and was left vulnerable and defenseless, and constantly needful of a strong father-figure. He was fortunate later in finding one in George Washington, but, naturally, even Washington could not supply the needed magic, and so in spite of Jefferson's veneration of Washington there was always an element of ambivalence in his feelings for him.

It may seem extraordinary that this greatly gifted man, so well-endowed by nature, should have felt the need of moral support. But the loss of one's father before one is through his adolescence can create a great emotional gap, which can never quite be filled by another, no matter how highly honored and successful the man may be. Many men spend their lives trying to compensate for this loss, and Jefferson was probably one of them. He could feel strong only in the presence of strong men. They lent him the backbone that he felt somehow was missing. But the events of Jefferson's life constantly pushed him into the position of a strong man, a position from which he periodically had to withdraw in order to give expression to his other passive, feminine, artistic side.

CHAPTER SIX

❧ ❦

Jefferson resigned his seat in Congress on the second of September 1776, and the next day he set out for Virginia. Although he had expressed a wish to withdraw from the Virginia Constitutional Convention, claiming his domestic situation made this move "indispensably necessary," he was nevertheless re-elected a member from his own county in October, and on the seventh he took his seat in the House of Delegates, that being the first day of the session.

On the second day a dispatch came for Jefferson from Congress in Philadelphia, informing him that he had been elected, along with Benjamin Franklin and Silas Dean, to the joint commission to represent the United States in Paris. He was almost irresistibly tempted to accept. The thought of working shoulder-to-shoulder with Franklin, whose diplomacy he so greatly valued, was an enticing one, as was the hope of winning France as a dependable ally. Added to these was an intoxicating vision of Paris—the celestial abode of the arts, where he knew he would immediately feel at home. But it was not to be. He kept the messenger waiting three days before he could get himself to say a final "No." The messenger rode away with Jefferson's answer to the President of Congress, which read thus:

"It would argue great insensibility to me, could I receive with indifference so confidential an appointment from your body. My thanks are a poor return for the partiality they have been pleased to entertain for me. No cares of my own person, nor yet for my private affairs, would have induced one moment's hesitation to accept the charge. But circumstances very peculiar in the situation of my family, such as neither permit me to leave nor to carry it, compel me to ask leave to decline a service so honorable, and, at the same time, so important to the American cause. The necessity under which I labor, and the conflict I have undergone for three days, during which I could not determine to dismiss your messenger, will, I hope, plead my pardon to Congress; and I am sure there are too many of that body to whom they may with better hopes confide this charge, to leave them under a moment's difficulty in making a new choice."

The circumstance to which he referred was, of course, the illness and enfeebled health of his wife. He could neither leave her nor take her with him, without endangering her life. But he seems to have been unable to say this in simple and direct words to the president of Congress. This was another example of his shyness, of his great reluctance to expose his personal life to public gaze. In such matters his reserve was colossal. Mrs. Jefferson was pregnant with her third child and only son, born May 28, 1777. During these periods, of which there were to be three more, she was often alarmingly ill both before and after the event. Her husband's account-book contains the following entry: "June 14. Our son died 10h. 20m. P.M." That was all.

Certainly one of the reasons for Jefferson's quitting Congress and taking his seat in the Virginia House of Burgesses was to stay in Monticello, where he could keep a solicitous and vigilant eye on his ailing wife, which would have been impossible in Philadelphia, or, of course, in Paris.

But there were other reasons, as well. He knew how much preparatory work had to be done before Virginia could be freed from her Royalist fetters and made ready to play the leading part she did play in the new nation. And he knew that in this process his own legal training would be of inestimable use. He was now ripe as a public man. His education had been greatly enhanced by the ordeal through which he had passed in defending, at least in his own mind, the Declaration of Independence against the attacks of his colleagues.

After July 4, little that he wrote needed such drastic pruning. He was buttressed by other Virginia liberals, among them Patrick Henry, now governor of the state, Edmund Pendleton, Henry's predecessor as governor, George Mason, who early set his face against slavery or any compromise with it, and George Wythe, Jefferson's former teacher and now close friend, an abolitionist who had freed his own slaves long before Virginia freed hers. To the list should be added James Madison, still but twenty-five, diminutive of stature, modest, unimposing, who shone neither in debate nor through his pen, but whose heart was wholly dedicated to his country. No one ranked higher in Jefferson's esteem and affection.

Jefferson came gradually to be recognized as leader of this group. To each of them he paid tribute with unstinting, selfless praise. George Mason he described, for example, as "a man of the first order of wisdom . . . of expansive mind, profound judgement, cogent in argument, learned in the lore of our former Constitution. . . ." "Mr. Pendleton, taken all in all, was the ablest man in debate I have ever met with . . . cool, smooth, and persuasive; his language flowing, chaste, and embellished. . . ." Jefferson added that Pendleton was also one of the most virtuous and benevolent men and the kindest of friends, amiable and pleasant as a companion. Mr. Wythe he extolled for "His pure integrity, judgement and reasoning," all of which gave him great weight. And Mr. Madison he praised for his self-possession, for "Never wandering from his subject into vain declamation, but pursuing it closely, in language pure, classical and copious. . . ." To be so warmly generous in the estimate of his close associates reflects a mind untrammeled by petty jealousies, and one that could express its thoughts with judicious precision.

On October 11, the day that the messenger left Williamsburg to return to Philadelphia bearing Jefferson's regrets, the governor brought in a bill establishing courts of justice in the commonwealth. Three days later came his bill abolishing entail and primogeniture and allowing a man to leave his property according to his own inclination. This was a severe blow to the landed gentry and did much to brand Thomas Jefferson as an unprincipled "demagogue" and to earn him the bitter hatred of the privileged classes. He learned early to suffer abuse in silence.

He sat successively on most of the important committees: to settle the disputed boundary line with Pennsylvania; to define the meaning of treason; to raise six battalions of infantry; to encourage domestic manufactures; to amend the ordinances in regard to naval affairs; and to take into consideration all matters related to religion and morality. In addition, he led an important minority in defense of religious freedom and enunciated principles later to be incorporated into the Bill of Rights. A majority of the citizens of Virginia were dissenters, he thought; but he realized that their representatives in the legislature belonged to the established church. In his *Notes on Virginia* he would soon write:

"The legitimate powers of government extend to such acts only as are injurious to others. But it does me no injury for my neighbor to say there are twenty gods, or no God. It neither picks my pocket nor breaks my leg. . . . Reason and free inquiry are the only effectual agents against error. . . . They are the natural enemies of error and of error only."

Most enlightened people would support Jefferson in this statement. Despite his idealism, he was quite aware of the dangers that lurked in a democracy. "It can never be too often repeated," he wrote, "that the time for fixing every essential right on a legal basis is while our rulers are honest, and ourselves united. From the conclusion of this war we shall be going down hill. It will not then be necessary to resort every moment to the people for support. They will be forgotten, therefore, and their rights disregarded. They will forget themselves, but in the sole faculty of making money, and will never think of uniting to effect a due respect for their rights. The shackles, therefore, which shall not be knocked off at the conclusion of this war, will remain on us long, will be made heavier and heavier, till our rights shall revive or expire in a convulsion."

In August of 1777 Jefferson wrote to Franklin in France:

"I wish my domestic situation had rendered it possible for me to join you in the very honorable charge confided to you. Residence in a polite Court, society of literati of the first order, a just cause and an approving God, will add length to a life for which all men pray and none more than your most humble and obedient servant. . . ."

At the same time he assured Franklin that the people of Virginia had laid aside the monarchical and taken up the republican form of government "with as much ease as would have attended their throwing off an old and putting on a new suit of clothes."

It is said that Jefferson kept no files of his letters before 1779, but that he managed to recover most of them from the persons to whom they had been addressed. In fact, until he reached France in 1784, there are relatively few copies of his personal letters extant. In France he found copying machines, and so from that time on he did preserve copies of many of his private letters. He was exceedingly precise and methodical in filing his personal papers. When he was an old man, a youthful visitor once called on him to inquire about a lawsuit in which his father had been involved—nearly a half-century before. Jefferson stepped to a case, took out a batch of ancient papers from a pigeonhole, and in less than a minute produced the desired document. This systematic trait in a man who was also by taste and temperament an artist is rare, especially as he was without the accompanying indecisiveness and ambivalence that so often plague an obsessional or compulsive worker. Yet his letters are not without their obsessional traits. In a long epistle addressed to Governor Patrick Henry, which, when printed, covers seven and a half octavo pages, obviously written in heat, but with great politeness, there were no fewer than thirty-eight substitutions and emendations, beginning with "Sir" in place of "May it please your Excellency." The letter concerned the disposition of British troops captured in Burgoyne's defeat at Saratoga and marched, after staying a year in Boston, seven hundred miles to Virginia—4,000 of them. Four thousand more mouths to feed, a fact which caused great consternation, almost panic, among the people of Albemarle, who demanded their removal. The governor was greatly disinclined to turn a deaf ear to popular demands. Jefferson, on the other hand, could look facts

in the face unflinchingly and marshaled his arguments with telling force. The march from Boston was in the dead of winter, accompanied by terrible hardships. As spring approached, the
troops were well installed; they had erected spacious barracks,
planted gardens, cultivated the fields, and brought in domestic
animals. Their officers had rented houses for themselves and re-
paired them at their own expense.

Jefferson's blood boiled at the cruelty and injustice of disrupt-
ing the contented state of the prisoners. Although gentle and indeed humble in his man-to-man relationships, he could become
greatly angered, not at another person, but at an idea. This
seemed safer to him and spared him the pain of direct conflict
with a fellow being.

He concluded his long letter to Governor Henry by saying:

"The separation of these troops would be a breach of public
faith, therefore I suppose it impossible. . . . the health of the
troops neglected, their wishes crossed and their comforts torn
from them, the character of whim and caprice or, what is worse,
of cruelty fixed on us as a nation, and to crown the whole our
own people disgusted with such a proceeding."

And then, perhaps feeling abashed at his outburst, or knowing
his man, he added: "I am sensible however that the same object
may appear to different persons in very different lights. What I
have urged as reasons may to sounder minds be apparent falla-
cies."

Patrick Henry was a kind-hearted, if impulsive, man. There
was no further talk of removing the prisoners. The English and
German generals, from the Baron de Riedesel down, were effu-
sive in their appreciation of Jefferson.

In characteristic wisdom and generosity, Jefferson wrote Major
General Phillips:

"The great cause which divides our countries is not to be decided by individual animosities. The harmony of private societies
cannot weaken national efforts. To contribute by neighborly intercourse and attention to make others happy, is the shortest and
surest way of being happy ourselves. As these sentiments seem to
have directed your conduct, we should be as unwise as illiberal,

were we not to preserve the same temper of mind."

Jefferson opened his house and library, and garden, and made available his musical instruments to the foreign officers. His warm hospitality won their hearts, and the Germans at least repaid him by sparing his property, in which act of gratitude the British, however, did not join.

Jefferson's extreme, almost unctuous, deference to the governor in the letter quoted above may indeed proclaim his sweet reasonableness, but it should be pointed out that Patrick Henry's term of office was drawing to a close after three years, and that Jefferson himself was Henry's logical successor.

He was, in fact, elected governor of Virginia on June 1, 1779, defeating by a very small margin John Page, his old friend and fellow student at William and Mary. Neither candidate had electioneered or pushed himself forward. Indeed, Page wrote Jefferson a letter of apology and congratulations, to which Jefferson replied:

"It had given me much pain that the zeal of our respective friends should ever have placed us in the situation of competitors. I was comforted, however, with the reflection, that it was their competition, not ours, and that the difference of the numbers which decided between us was too insignificant to give you a pain or me a pleasure, had our dispositions towards each other been such as to admit those sensations."

He was thirty-six years old when he began his administration. The territory which Jefferson was called upon to govern embraced all of Virginia, West Virginia, and Kentucky, besides a great part of what is now Ohio, Indiana, and Illinois—a region that swarmed with brave and warlike Indians. In fact, Virginia was soon threatened at all points of the compass, while General Washington was demanding everything it had of arms, food, men, and money. This was the task that confronted a young lawyer "with a talent for music, a taste for art, a love of science, literature and gardening." In Washington's view, this was the most gloomy period through which the young country had yet passed. Virginia had almost no defensive strength—only one gun to four or five militiamen, according to Jefferson's calculations—with an enormous expanse of territory (over sixty thousand square miles) very thinly populated, and nakedly exposed to attack by heavily armed British vessels from the waters of both Chesapeake Bay and the James. Virginia's 270,000 slaves, most of them loyal but constantly cajoled and threatened by the enemy, required continuous watching.

By the time Governor Jefferson took office, the British scheme for conquering the South had already been put into operation. Savannah was taken in December 1778, and Georgia quickly fell. South Carolina had been entered, and Charleston was severely menaced. In Virginia, a large amount of public and private property had been destroyed and pillaged. Perhaps the only good news came from the west, where George Rogers Clarke turned the tide against General Hamilton and took him prisoner. The Governor's Council then advised him to put the prisoner and his two officers in irons, confine them in a dungeon of the public jail, forbid them the use of pen and paper and all communication except with their keeper.

The previous October, Congress had declared to the world that "Considering themselves bound to love their enemies," they had *"studied* to spare those who were in arms against them, and to lighten the chains of captivity."

This is just what Jefferson had done with Burgoyne's men basking in the hospitality of Albemarle County. But Jefferson, though humane and gentle by nature, was not soft. He kept the prisoners in their dark, chill, and repulsive underground dungeon reeking of rotten straw, until a letter of protest came from General Phillips, himself a prisoner of war in a comfortable house near Monticello. Phillips argued that Hamilton had surrendered and should therefore be treated as a prisoner of war. Jefferson was perplexed as to the correct line of his duty. He laid the matter before General Washington. The result was the removal of the prisoners' shackles and their admission to parole.

But such civilities did not alter the swelling tide of events. In April 1780, the state capital removed from Williamsburg to Richmond, the government finding shelter in temporary wooden structures. A letter then came to Jefferson from Madison, stating that Washington's army was on the verge of dissolution, being short of bread and nearly out of meat. "Scarce a week, and sometimes scarce a day, but brings us a most lamentable picture from Head Quarters. The Army are a great part of their time on short allowance. . . . General Washington has found it of the utmost difficulty to repress the mutinous spirit engendered by hunger and want of pay." Such was the news assailing the governor's ears. A British fleet and army were investing Charleston, the army moving northward over North Carolina into Virginia.

Jefferson was by now thoroughly aroused. He wrote General Washington on October 8, 1779:

"I shall give immediate orders for having in readiness every engine which the Enemy have contrived for the destruction of our unhappy citizens captivated by them. The presentiment of these operations is shocking beyond expression. I pray heaven to avert them: but nothing in this world will do it but a proper conduct of the Enemy. In every event I shall resign myself to the hard necessity under which I shall act."

Jefferson had no choice; the enemy was forcing his hand. In his man-to-man relationships he remained cool and humble. However, his anger, not directed at another person but sublimated into an idea, could become terrible indeed. This was an important attribute of his character. His mind kept silently working over various impulses and ideas, trying to render them acceptable, without slipping into the depression which seemed often to lie in wait for him.

CHAPTER SEVEN

Jefferson was by now forewarned of the defenselessness of Virginia. He was without funds and, as he told Washington, there was not a single man among the troops he hoped to raise who had ever seen the face of an enemy. In such circumstances it was to be expected that the governor would be blamed by his fellow Virginians for doing too much and, at the same time, for not doing enough in protecting his own state. Whatever the truth, there can be no doubt of his unwavering support of General Washington. His need of a strong man behind him was greater than ever. Washington was well aware of the perilous situation, especially after the incursions of the "parricide" (Jefferson's word), Benedict Arnold.

The summer of 1780 was a time of tireless activity on Jefferson's part. He stimulated the recruiting system, wrote letters urging the use of the rapidly deteriorating currency, and made every effort to get out the last man with the last dollar while it still had any value. All the supplies and equipment he could beg, buy, or borrow were immediately shipped south to General Gates's headquarters in North Carolina, for Jefferson realized that the only chance he had of keeping Cornwallis at bay was to strengthen Gates's hand. Not only were supplies such as metal, canvas, and leather giving out, but there were no wagons to be had for transporting them.

In the midst of this desperate situation, General Gates suffered his disastrous defeat at Camden on August 16, 1780. Within a few months, the British fleet had entered the James and had come to anchor at Jamestown, just seven miles from Williamsburg. Jefferson received a dispatch announcing the fact that the enemy had landed troops at Westover, twenty-five miles distant. He now found himself alone; not a member of the council remained in Richmond to help him. His wife and three children, the youngest but two months old, were sent to the house of a relative at Tucka-hoe, Virginia.

Jefferson mounted his horse and took command. He directed that all matériel should be conveyed across or dumped into the river so that Arnold could not lay hands on it. Overseeing this work, first at Richmond, then at Westham, Jefferson reached Tuckahoe at one in the morning. There he helped his family across the river and saw them to a safer refuge eight miles upstream. Galloping back to a point opposite Westham, he resumed direction of the transfer of public property. Before he reached Manchester, opposite Richmond, his horse sank under him from exhaustion and died on the road. Jefferson then placed the saddle and bridle on his own back and stopped at the next farmhouse, where he borrowed an unbroken colt. Within sight of Richmond, he found that the enemy was already in possession of it.

Arnold remained in Richmond for only twenty-three hours— long enough, however, to destroy tons of tobacco and powder and to spoil at least three hundred muskets. By a lucky change in the wind, which carried him swiftly down the river, he managed to escape ahead of the twenty-five hundred militia at his heels.

After forty-eight hours in the saddle, Governor Jefferson returned to the capital, where he offered a reward for Arnold's capture. But the traitor was too wary to be trapped.

In the midst of chaos and a fatal want of arms, Jefferson did what he could to support Generals Greene, Lafayette, and Steuben against the depredations of Arnold, Cornwallis, Phillips, and Tarleton.

Although the legislature conferred absolute powers upon the governor, authorizing him to call out the whole militia, to impress all wagons, horses, food, clothing, supplies, and slaves, Jefferson was in fact powerless without arms. His term as governor was drawing to a close—to his relief, because of his constant worry about his wife. But his troubles were far from over. General Tarleton was advancing swiftly toward Charlottesville. As his dragoons swept by the Cuckoo Tavern in Louisa, a citizen named Jouitte, suspecting their destination to be Monticello, mounted his thoroughbred and rode at top speed by a little-known and shorter route to announce the imminent arrival of the British troops. He reached Monticello a little before sunrise and informed the governor of the peril he was in.

Tarleton had dispatched a troop under Captain McLeod to proceed to Monticello and capture the governor. Fortunately, an emissary arrived bringing word to Jefferson that the British were already ascending the mountain. Jefferson then sent his wife and children off in a carriage to a point fourteen miles distant. For nearly two hours he busied himself by securing his most important papers and then ordered his favorite saddle horse to be brought from Shadwell Ford, where it was being shod. Taking his telescope in hand, Jefferson set out on foot for the place where he was to meet his horse. From a rock on Carter's Mountain, he got a good view of Charlottesville, but at first could see nothing alarming. He then noticed, in kneeling down to look through his telescope, that his light walking-sword had slipped from its sheath. In going back to retrieve it, he took another look and saw the streets of the town swarming with dragoons. Now, for the first time, he mounted his horse and followed after his family.

Within five minutes of the time he had left his house, McLeod entered it. He had strict orders from Tarleton to disturb nothing of Mr. Jefferson's possessions. Two faithful slaves, Martin and Caesar, who were left in the house, were busy hiding silver and other valuables under the floor of the front portico. Martin stood above and handed the articles down to Caesar. As the last piece went in, Martin caught a glimpse through the trees of the white coats of the dragoons. He immediately lowered the plank and shut Caesar up in the dark hole below. There he remained without food or light for eighteen hours.

Martin thereupon received Captain McLeod with great dignity and showed him through the house. On reaching Jefferson's study, McLeod looked about him and then locked the door, giving Martin the key. Within eighteen hours Captain McLeod withdrew from Monticello. All these facts were handed down in the Jefferson family and were repeatedly heard from Jefferson's lips.

In contrast to the handsome behavior of the British under Tarleton at Monticello was their conduct under Cornwallis at Elk Hill, Jefferson's James River estate, which they laid waste. They destroyed all his growing crops of corn and tobacco, burned his farms, and used his whole stock of cattle, sheep, and hogs for the sustenance of Cornwallis's army. They carried off all horses capable of service and cut the throats of the colts, in the meanwhile burning all the fences on the plantation. They carried off about thirty slaves. "Had this been to give them freedom," Jefferson wrote in his farm book, "he [Cornwallis] would have done right, but it was to consign them to inevitable death from the small-pox and putrid fever then raging in his camp." And he added, "History will never relate the horrors committed by the British army in the Southern States of America." All the above facts were recorded in detail in Mr. Jefferson's farm book.

At the end of the second year of his term of office, Jefferson resigned his position as governor, which he had the right to do, although there was no imperative need. On June 8, 1781, George Washington closed a letter to Jefferson with these words:

"Allow me, before I take leave of your Excellency in your public capacity, *to express the obligations I am under for the readiness and zeal with which you have always forwarded and supported every measure, which I have had occasion to recommend through you,* and to assure you that I shall esteem myself honored by a continuation of your friendship and correspondence, should your country permit you to remain in the private walk of life."

Jefferson had no choice except to resign. The state of his wife's health was a source of constant anxiety to him. He promised her that when he quit public office on this occasion he would never again leave her to take part in political life. He felt, moreover, that under the pressure of invasion the public would have more confidence in a military chief, and this too influenced him in his decision to take advantage of his constitutional right to retire after two years in office. In any case, he seems to have had no wish to continue in office, whatever his real reasons were for quitting. Was he perhaps on the edge of a depression which led him to withdraw from public life?

For twelve days Virginia had no governor. The legislature had now fled four times before Arnold's advancing troops. It came to rest at Staunton, forty miles west of Charlottesville, and here it blamed Jefferson for not having called out the militia. There was a strong movement afoot to name Patrick Henry dictator. This Jefferson called "treason against the people, . . . treason against mankind in general," and he threw his weight in favor of Thomas Nelson, the commander-in-chief of the state militia, who was duly elected and given absolute powers. Nelson had the mixed satisfaction of sending cannonballs crashing through his own dining room at Yorktown, where British officers were making merry over glasses of his best wine.

For tactical reasons, Jefferson had kept his intended resignation secret from the House; but once it was announced and Henry's ambitions were quashed, there was a burst of feeling in favor of Jefferson and an insistence on his re-election.

During all the disputes and arguments about the propriety of Jefferson's conduct in office, he remained quietly at Poplar Forest, far from the legislature. According to his custom, he did not attempt to influence its proceedings either. But being a sensitive and in many respects an introverted man, he took the implied criticism deeply to heart and, indeed, brooded over it for many months. "No slave," he wrote, "was so wretched as 'the minister of a commonwealth.' " For him the rebuke came just at the wrong time, when his estate was overrun and falling to pieces, when many of his servants had been abducted or had died, and when his family had been driven from their home, all because of his own faithful dedication to public duty. He was not only unhappy but indignant, so much so that he resolved to forswear public service forever and to return to the legislature just once more to face his accusers. He was to repeat this pattern several times in his political career.

In the spring of 1781 he had been asked by the president of Congress to serve, with Benjamin Franklin, John Jay, and Henry Laurens, in joining John Adams at the expected negotiations for peace in Paris. This invitation lent a temporary lift to his spirits, although, he said, to decline it gave him more mortification than almost any occurrence of his life. "I lose an opportunity," he wrote Lafayette from Monticello on August 4, 1781, "the only one I ever had and perhaps ever shall have of combining public service with private gratification, of seeing count[ries] whose improvements in science, in arts, and in civilization it has been my fortune to [ad]mire at a distance but never to see. . . ."

He might indeed have gone but for the show of legislative censure. He was far too proud and honorable to turn tail under fire. It was perhaps no accident that a month earlier, in the midst of so many disheartening events, including the death of his infant son, he had accidentally fallen from his horse and suffered severe contusions. These confined him to his house, but not to his bed. It was during this period that he wrote his famous *Notes on Virginia*. Parenthetically, it should be mentioned that the doctor who called to see him twice charged him six hundred pounds. In the same week Jefferson's account-book shows that he paid fifty pounds for chicken and £71 2s. for three quarts of brandy.

On October 19, largely because of French maritime intervention, Cornwallis surrendered at Yorktown, and almost eight thousand British troops laid down their arms. This, of course, rejoiced the hearts of all Virginians.

Jefferson had been re-elected to his seat as a member of the Virginia legislature from Albemarle County. He was ready to meet and answer any charges against him. The House of Delegates held its hearing on December 19. His accuser was absent. There was silence in the chamber. Jefferson rose to make his reply, whereupon the General Assembly unanimously extended its sincere thanks to the former governor and expressed in the strongest manner the high opinion of "Mr. Jefferson's Ability, Rectitude, and Integrity, as cheif [*sic*] Magistrate of this Commonwealth . . . thus publicly avowing their Opinion to obviate *all future* and to remove all *former* unmerited Censure."

But even this balm did not heal the wound. Jefferson had already left Poplar Forest in August and returned to Monticello. From the French legation in Philadelphia he had received a request for factual information about the state of Virginia. His answers were included in his *Notes on Virginia,* which were published in the winter of 1782. For almost anyone else this would have been a monumental task; but he was so punctilious, so everlastingly persistent in his note-taking and recordings, that he turned out a document of enduring value in a short time. It was based on a vast amount of personal observation and statistical material. Can one doubt that he threw himself into this work partly to help him recover from his depressed feelings?

When spring came he had already made up his mind to withdraw from public life. He shunned the session of the legislature. James Monroe wrote him a polite remonstrance, saying that he should not decline service to his country. In Jefferson's reply, dated May 20, 1782, he said that he was always mortified when anything was expected of him that he could not fulfill, especially if it related to public service. But he went on:

"Before I ventured to declare to my countrymen my determination to retire from public employment I examined well my heart to know whether it were thoroughly cured of every principle of political ambition, whether no lurking particle remained which might leave me uneasy when reduced within the limits of mere private life. I became satisfied that every fibre of that passion was thoroughly eradicated. I examined also in other views my right to withdraw. I considered that I had been thirteen years engaged in public service, that during that time I had so totally abandoned all attention to my private affairs as to permit them to run into great disorder and ruin. . . ."

He continued by saying that the only reward he ever wanted was the affection of his countrymen, but that the disapprobation of their representatives was a shock on which he had not calculated. In spite of their declared exculpation, he felt that the inju-

ries he had received at the hands of his peers "had inflicted a
wound on my spirit which will only be cured by the all-healing
grave."

Monroe was fifteen years Jefferson's junior, and Jefferson stood
as adviser, mentor, and political father to him. In view of his
great reluctance to display his intimate personal feelings, it is remarkable that he was willing to reveal so much to Monroe; but of
course he could not mention what must have been uppermost in
his mind—the dreadful suspense over his wife's rapid decline and
what was obvious to him: that he could under no circumstances
leave her.

Mrs. Jefferson died on September 6, 1782, at quarter to twelve
in the morning, leaving him with three daughters—Martha, age
ten; Mary, age four; and Lucy, just four months old, who lived
only into her second year. The births and deaths of his children
were recorded in Jefferson's hand in his prayer book.

After Martha Jefferson's death, their daughter Martha was Jefferson's constant companion. She left this account of her father
during this tragic time of his life:

"As a nurse, no female ever had more tenderness or anxiety. He
nursed my poor mother in turn with Aunt Carr and her own
sister—sitting up with her and administering her medicines and
drink to the last. For four months that she lingered, he was never
out of calling; when not at her bedside, he was writing in a small
room which opened immediately at the head of her bed. A moment before the closing scene, he was led from the room almost in
a state of insensibility by his sister, Mrs. Carr, who, with great difficulty, got him into his library, where he fainted, and remained
so long insensible that they feared he never would revive. The
scene that followed I did not witness; but the violence of his emo-
tion, when almost by stealth I entered his room at night, to this
day I dare not trust myself to describe. He kept his room three
weeks, and I was never a moment from his side. He walked almost incessantly night and day, only lying down occasionally,
when nature was completely exhausted, on a pallet that had been
brought in during his long fainting fit. My aunts remained con-

stantly with him for some weeks, I do not remember how many. When at last he left his room, he rode out, and from that time he was incessantly on horseback, rambling about the mountain, in the least frequented roads, and just as often through the woods. In those melancholy rambles, I was his constant companion, a solitary witness to many a violent burst of grief, the remembrance of which has consecrated particular scenes of that lost home beyond the power of time to obliterate."

A month after his wife's death, Jefferson addressed a letter to her sister, saying that he found himself absolutely unable to attend to anything like business.

"This miserable kind of existence," he wrote, "is really too burthensome to be borne, and were it not for the infidelity of deserting the sacred charge left me, I could not wish it's continuance a moment. For what could it be wished? All my plans of comfort and happiness reversed by a single event and nothing answering in prospect before me but a gloom unbrightened with one chearful expectation. The care and instruction of our children indeed affords some temporary abstractions from wretchedness and nourishes a soothing reflection that if there be beyond the grave any concern for the things of this world there is one angel at least who views these attentions with pleasure and wishes continuance of them while she must pity the miseries to which they confine me."

On November 26, 1782, nearly three months after he suffered his tragic loss, Jefferson wrote his friend the Marquis of Chastellux, saying that he was "a little emerging from that stupor of mind which had rendered me as dead to the world as she was whose loss occasioned it."

Although none of his letters to his wife or hers to him were preserved for posterity to gaze upon, in the most secret drawer of a private cabinet were found, forty-four years after Jefferson's death, envelopes containing locks of his wife's hair and other souvenirs, all labeled and arranged in perfect order, but giving evidence of having been much handled.

Perhaps a few days before her death, part in her handwriting and part in his, together they wrote these lines from *Tristram Shandy:*

"Time wastes too fast: every letter
I trace tells me with what rapidity
life follows my pen. The days and hours
of it are flying over our heads like
clouds of windy day never to return—
more every thing presses on—and every
time I kiss thy hand to bid adieu, every absence which
follows it, are preludes to that eternal separation
which we are shortly to make!"

Over her grave, near that of his sister Jane and his dear friend
Dabney Carr and the graves of the infants they had lost, is a
plain, horizontal slab of white marble bearing these words:

"To the memory of
Martha Jefferson,
Daughter of John Wayles;
Born October 19th, 1748, O.S.
Intermarried with
Thomas Jefferson
January 1st, 1772;
Torn from him by death
September 6th 1782:
This monument of his love is inscribed."

And then two lines in Greek letters from the *Iliad,* which,
translated, would read:

"Though the dead forget their dead with Hades in the grave
Even there I shall remember my sweet friend." *

Poor Jefferson; he had lost half of himself. It was natural for
him to withdraw from public life and to bury himself in his grief,

---

* "Εἰ δὲ θανόντων περ καταλήθοντ' ειν Αἰδαο,
Αὐτὰρ ἐγὼ κἀκεῖθί φίλη μεμνήσομ' ἑταίρϑ."
Translation in John Dos Passos, *The Head and Heart of Thomas Jefferson*
(New York: Doubleday, 1954), p. 249.

which was not unmixed with bitterness. Although he felt hurt and desperate and deprived, and had suffered a great loss, he was not one to revel in martyrdom for long. Indeed, he began, after his suffering, gradually to recover and again to contemplate the distant possibilities of his career.

CHAPTER EIGHT

❧ ❀ ❧

In late November 1782, Jefferson went with his children to Ampthill, the estate in Chesterfield County of his friend Colonel Archibald Cary, who had offered his house to him so that the children and their cousins, the Carrs, could be inoculated for smallpox. The method then used was called variolation, or the inoculation of pustular material from a patient suffering from the disease. It was obviously not without its dangers, but fourteen years would have to elapse before the safer method of vaccination with cow pox would be ready for use at Dr. Edward Jenner's hands in Berkeley, England. It would not be until 1802 that Dr. Benjamin Waterhouse would introduce vaccination into America. Jefferson was to become one of its enthusiastic sponsors. In fact, in that year, when he was president of the United States, he wrote a letter to Jenner from Monticello acknowledging the receipt of a copy of his writings.

"Having been among the early converts, in this part of the globe, to its efficiency, I took an early part in recommending it to my countrymen. I avail myself of this occasion of rendering you a portion of the tribute of gratitude due to you from the whole human family. Medicine has never before produced any single improvement of such utility. . . . You have erased from the calendar of human afflictions one of its greatest. Yours is the comfortable reflection that mankind can never forget that you have lived.

Future nations will know by history only that the loathsome small-pox has existed and by you has been extirpated."

While Jefferson and his children were at Ampthill, he received a letter from Robert R. Livingston of New York, then secretary of foreign affairs. The letter was marked "Philadelphia, 13th. Novr. 1782"; it read:

"Sir, I have the honor to transmit a resolution of Congress, appointing you one of their Ministers Plenipotentiary for negociating a peace. I rejoice in this fresh proof of their confidence in your Virtue and abilities. The sacrifices you have heretofore made to the interests of your Country, induce me to hope that you will suffer no personal consideration to prevent their being employed in its service upon this important occasion."

Enclosed in this letter was a copy of the Resolution signed by Charles Thomson, the secretary of Congress, stating that it was a renewal of the appointment offered to Jefferson a year and a half earlier.

Within two weeks Jefferson wrote to Livingston from Chesterfield assuring him that he would lose no moment in preparing for his departure. He had hoped to sail with Comte de Rochambeau and the Marquis de Chastellux, but the vessel which carried them left the port before he could be ready. So he informed Benjamin Franklin and John Jay in separate letters, both written on January 3, 1783.

Apparently Jefferson's appointment had been agreed upon unanimously in Congress without a single adverse remark. Before this appointment came to him he had thought he had "folded" himself "in the arms of retirement, and rested all prospects of future happiness on domestic and literary objects," as he wrote Chastellux. And elsewhere he wrote: "I had two months before that, lost the cherished companion of my life, in whose affections, unabated on both sides, I had lived the last ten years in unchequered happiness. With the public interests, the state of my mind concurred in recommending the change of scene proposed; and I accepted the appointment. . . ."

But there were to be many delays. The enemy's fleet had blockaded the port of Baltimore. And then came the news that the preliminaries to a peace treaty had been signed. Thereupon Congress informed him that affairs were so far advanced that there was no longer a need of his going. He left his two younger children with their aunt, Mrs. Eppes, and placed Martha, then eleven years old, at school in Philadelphia. He returned to Monticello, but he soon found himself in Trenton and then Annapolis, where Congress had assembled in November, on the twenty-sixth. He had been elected a delegate by the general assembly of Virginia the previous June.

Now began a series of letters to his children—principally to Martha, whom he called Patsy. They are tender, maternal; but humorless, and obviously anxious and conditional, at least in their expressions of his love.

"Annapolis Nov. 28, 1783.

My dear Patsy,

After four days' journey, I arrived here without any accident, and in as good health as when I left Philadelphia. The conviction that you would be more improved in the situation I have placed you than if still with me, has solaced me on my parting with you, which my love for you has rendered a difficult thing. The acquirements which I hope you will make under the tutors I have provided for you will render you more worthy of my love; and if they can not increase it, they will prevent its diminution. . . . With respect to the distribution of your time, the following is what I should approve:

From 8 to 10, practice music.

From 10 to 1, dance one day and draw another.

From 1 to 2, draw on the day you dance, and write a letter next day.

From 3 to 4, read French.

From 4 to 5, exercise yourself in music.

From 5 till bed-time, read English, write, etc."

He urged her to communicate this plan to Mrs. Hopkinson, the lady to whom he had entrusted her care. And he added several other directives: to write him by every post, to inform him what books she read, and what tunes she learned, to write one letter a week to each of her three aunts and to her little sister Mary. Then he said, "Take care that you never spell a word wrong. . . . It produces great praise to a lady to spell well."

From our vantage point, Jefferson himself made many mistakes in spelling.

He closed the letter with these admonitions, which must have been a burden, even to the most dutiful child.

"I have placed my happiness on seeing you good and accomplished; and no distress which this world can now bring on me would equal that of your disappointing my hopes. If you love me, then strive to be good under every situation and to all living creatures, and to acquire those accomplishments which I have put in your power, and which will go far towards ensuring you the warmest love of your affectionate father."

And then, to pile on the guilt, he added by way of postscript: "Keep my letters and read them at times, that you may always have present in your mind those things which will endear you to me."

A fortnight later he wrote that he hoped she would have good sense enough "to disregard those foolish predictions that the world is to be at an end soon. [Apparently there had been some earth tremors, which gave rise to this rumor.] The Almighty has never made known to any body at what time he created it; nor will he tell any body when he will put an end to it, if he ever means to do it. As to preparations for that event, the best way is for you always to be prepared for it. The only way to be so is, never to say or do a bad thing."

Then follows a homily on conscience, "this faithful internal monitor" which our Maker has given all of us and which should always be obeyed, in order to be prepared for the end of the world.

Within another two weeks he wrote Martha advising her about her dress

". . . which I know you are a little apt to neglect. I do not wish you to be gaily clothed at this time of life, but that your wear should be fine of its kind. But above all things and at all times let your clothes be neat, whole, and properly put on. Do not fancy you must wear them till the dirt is visible to the eye. . . . Nothing is so disgusting to our sex as a want of cleanliness and delicacy in yours. I hope, therefore, the moment you rise from bed, your first work will be to dress yourself in such style, as that you may be seen by any gentleman without his being able to discover a pin amiss, or any other circumstance of neatness wanting."

His letters to Patsy betray his worrisomeness—if not his despondent and lonesome state of mind. Under such circumstances, as one might guess, he kept himself endlessly occupied.

He was chairman of the Congressional committees to revise the currency, in which he was the first to recommend the dollar and its present subdivisions. It was Gouverneur Morris, however, who introduced the decimal into the American monetary system. Jefferson was also chairman of a "grand committee" to apportion the public debt among the states. He executed the deed for the cession of the Northwest Territory. In fact, he had headed nearly all the most important committees and was twice elected president of Congress *pro tem* in the absence of the president.

He has left a brief commentary on the House of Representatives:

"Our body was little numerous, but very contentious. Day after day was wasted on the most unimportant questions. A member, one of those afflicted with the morbid rage of debate, of an ardent mind, prompt imagination, and copious flow of words, who heard with impatience any logic which was not his own, sitting near me on some occasion of a trifling but wordy debate, asked me how I could sit in silence, hearing so much false reasoning, which a word should refute? I observed to him, that to refute indeed was easy, but to silence was impossible. . . . If the present Congress errs in too much talking, how can it be otherwise, in a body to which the people send one hundred and fifty lawyers, whose trade it is to question everything, yield nothing, and talk by the hour? That one hundred and fifty lawyers should do business together, ought not to be expected."

By contrast, Jefferson was a silent man, a listener who encouraged others to express their views. He was not given to controversy. His conviction was that every man has a right to his own opinion on all subjects and that others were bound to respect that right.

He once wrote his grandson:

"I never yet saw an instance of one of two disputants convincing the other by argument. I have seen many, of their getting warm, becoming rude, and shooting one another. Conviction is the effect of our own dispassionate reasoning, either in solitude, or weighing within ourselves, dispassionately, what we hear from others, standing uncommitted in argument ourselves. It was one of the rules, which, above all others, made Dr. Franklin the most amiable of men in society, 'never to contradict anybody.' "

The Marquis de Chastellux has left a fine description of his friend Thomas Jefferson:

"A man, not yet forty, tall and with a mild and pleasing countenance, but whose mind and understanding are ample substitutes for every exterior grace. An American, who, without ever having quitted his own country, is at once a musician, skilled in drawing, a geometrician, an astronomer, a natural philosopher, legislator, and statesman. . . . The visit which I made him was not unexpected, for he had long since invited me to come and pass a few days with him in the centre of the mountains; notwithstanding which, I found his appearance serious—nay even cold, but before I had been two hours with him, we were as intimate as if we had passed our whole lives together . . . a conversation always varied and interesting, always supported by the sweet satisfaction experienced by two persons, who, in communicating their sentiments and opinions are invariably in unison, and who understand each other at the first hint, made four days pass away like so many minutes. . . . It seemed as if from his youth he had placed his mind, as he had done his house on an elevated situation, from which he might contemplate the universe."

On May 7, 1784, Jefferson received his appointment from Congress as minister plenipotentiary, to serve with Adams and Franklin for the purpose of negotiating commercial treaties with foreign nations. Four days later he left Annapolis for Philadelphia, there to pick up his daughter Patsy, who was to accompany him. The two younger girls, as has been said, he had entrusted to the care of their maternal aunt, Mrs. Eppes; and his nephew, Peter Carr, the son of "the dearest friend I knew," Dabney Carr, was left as a "tender legacy" in the guardianship of James Madison.

On July 5, Jefferson and his daughter sailed from the port of Boston on the merchant ship *Ceres* bound for Cowes in England. Since the Fourth fell on Sunday, the celebration was deferred to the next day. Just about the time the *Ceres* weighed anchor and set sail, the Declaration of Independence was read aloud in Faneuil Hall. There were only six passengers aboard the *Ceres*. The voyage was a pleasant one and took only nineteen days. They landed at Portsmouth, where they were detained for a week because of little Martha's illness. She had become so dreadfully seasick toward the end of the voyage that she had to take to her bed. But she had written to friends in Philadelphia: "We had a lovely passage in a beautiful new ship, that had made but one passage before. There were only six passengers, all of whom Papa knew, and a fine sunshine all the way, with a sea which was as calm as a river." Finally they embarked for Le Havre and reached Paris on August 6.

Jefferson was enchanted with the French countryside. His experienced eye missed nothing. The rich fat fields reminded him of his own Virginia; the neat farms delighted him. He wrote Monroe that "nothing can be more fertile, better cultivated & more elegantly improved." In spite of this, the travelers were shocked by the misery and squalor they encountered. Martha wrote a friend:

"We should have had a very delightful voyage to Paris . . . through the most beautiful country I ever saw in my life—it is a perfect garden—if the singularity of our carriage (a phaeton) had not attracted the attention of all we met; and whenever we stopped we were surrounded by beggars—one day I counted no less than nine where we stopped to change horses."

Martha, still only twelve, seems to have acquired early in life her father's observing eye and facility of expression.

Jefferson soon took residence in a handsome house that had been procured for him. He was accompanied by his private secretary, William Short, and by Colonel David Humphreys, the secretary of the American legation. After a brief period of sightseeing,

Martha was placed in a convent school nearby.

Jefferson then called on Dr. Franklin at Passy. The old gentleman had applied for permission to return home. But this was not to be; instead, Jefferson was charged with the formidable task of assisting in drafting treaties with twenty foreign powers, to be accomplished in two years. The commissioners were cautioned against extravagance. Their allowance was reduced from eleven thousand dollars to nine thousand per year. Franklin commented:

"I commend their economy, and shall imitate it by diminishing my expense. Our too liberal entertainment of our countrymen here has been reported at home by our guests, to our disadvantage, and has given offence. They must be contented for the future, as I am, with plain beef and pudding. . . . For my own part, if I could sit down to dinner on a piece of their excellent salt pork and pumpkin, I would not give a farthing for all the luxuries of Paris."

Three weeks after Jefferson's arrival, Adams, who was in England and had been sent for, came to Passy for the first meeting of the three commissioners. They determined to meet every day until their business was concluded. They announced their mission to various ambassadors and prepared the draft of a treaty which they considered reasonable. It has been described as "the first serious attempt ever made to conduct the intercourse of nations on Christian principles." In short, although it contained twenty-seven articles, it was a human and humane document—such as one might expect from three such rational and serious men. It conceded the right of man to come and go, buy and sell, according to his own interest, "subject only to the laws of the country" he was in. It provided for the protection of shipwrecked mariners, who were not to be plundered and who were to be given decent burial if they died under foreign jurisdiction. The commissioners did what they could "to confine the evils of war, as much as possible, to belligerents. [How far we have fallen away from the wisdom of these three great Americans!] No molestation of fishermen, farmers, or other non-combatants. No confiscation of neutral property. No ravaging an enemy's coast. No seizure of vessels or other property for purposes of war. No crowding of prisoners of war into unwholesome places." When General Washington read the terms of the treaty drawn up in Dr. Franklin's house in Passy, in 1784, he said that it marked "a new era in negotiation."

The commissioners next sounded out various ambassadors then resident in Paris. "Old Frederick of Prussia," as Jefferson called him, "met us cordially and without hesitation," and with him a treaty was soon concluded. Denmark and Tuscany also entered into negotiations, but the other powers appeared indifferent. In fact, according to Jefferson, they seemed to know little about the United States except as rebels who had been successful in throwing off the yoke of the mother country. Napoleon Bonaparte was still a youth of sixteen, but would soon trample on every principle of humanity that the treaty hoped to secure.

On May 2, 1785, Jefferson received from Congress a document appointing him minister plenipotentiary to reside at the court of His Most Christian Majesty for three years. It was signed by John Jay, then secretary of foreign affairs, and Richard Henry Lee, the president of Congress. When the Count de Vergennes announced this appointment to Jefferson, saying to him, "You replace Dr. Franklin," Jefferson replied, "I succeed; no one can replace him."

On the twelfth of July, Dr. Franklin left Passy. All the neighborhood and a host of friends gathered to wish him well. The queen sent her own traveling-litter, a kind of sedan chair carried between two mules, to convey the grand old man to Le Havre. Jefferson said that it seemed "as if the village had lost its patriarch."

Franklin's wit and learning, his wisdom and diplomacy, had won the hearts of French men and women at all levels of society. Soon the close bond of admiration and affection that united the two Americans worked to Jefferson's advantage. The mantle of Franklin fell upon Jefferson's shoulders, and he too became immensely popular with the French, largely because of his urbanity, his taste, his solid intellectual attainments, and his philosophic and aesthetic interests. Not being a seasoned diplomatist, he often talked freely, with earnest warmth and a lack of conventional reserve. This too appealed to the French, who were beginning to look toward America for a model for themselves. Jefferson fell into no such misunderstandings as had strained the relationship between Franklin and the impetuous and often pugnaciously irritable Adams. In fact, Jefferson had the deepest respect and admiration for the New Englander, which was fully reciprocated. He always deferred to Adams, asked his opinion first and was tactful enough to urge him to take the post of honor. No doubt Abigail Adams's feelings enhanced and warmed her husband's. She had written home to her sister describing Thomas Jefferson as one of "the chosen of the earth."

Jefferson's concerns in Paris were confined to a few items: the receipt on favorable terms of whale oils, salted meat and fish; and of rice on terms equal to those given Piedmont, Egypt, and the Levant; and, above all, some mitigation of the tobacco monopoly. He found the French government disposed to friendship and fair dealings. The two envoys disagreed about the treatment of Barbary pirates who had captured the American brig *Betsy* and taken her crew to Morocco, where they were being held for ransom. Adams was for tribute; Jefferson for war. They wrote home for instructions. What Jefferson was advocating was a small navy to protect the freedom of the seas. Congress agreed with Adams, and there followed long negotiations which did not prevent the yearly increase of American captives in the prisons and slave markets of the Barbary Coast.

In the midst of his many diplomatic duties, Jefferson never lost interest in his native state. He made all arrangements for procuring a' statue of General Washington and selected Jean-Antoine Houdon to execute it. He watched each succeeding step until the completed sculpture was sent home to be erected in Richmond.

He was deeply persuaded that an agrarian society of independent farmers was the only safeguard against the corruption and moral depravity that he found so widespread in Europe. And he was suspicious of factory workers, or what he called "the class of artificers" who, he believed, would wreck the hopes of mankind in liberty and self-government. It was not that mechanical occupations in themselves led to vice. There was no one more partial to such conveniences and labor-saving devices than he was, but he distrusted great aggregations of ignorant, impoverished factory operatives, living in squalor under the domination of corrupt and powerful employers. This he had observed in France and later in England and hoped never to see in America.

The existence of a large and affluent middle class had not yet shaped the destiny of America. He must have seen what the future held, however, for he had written Washington:

"All the world is becoming commercial. . . . Our citizens have had too full a taste of the comforts furnished by the arts & manufactures to be debarred the use of them. We must then in our defence endeavour to share as large a portion as we can of this modern source of wealth & power."

He himself, however, had no taste for trade. He believed that only a man who owned his own acres and worked in the open air could be really free and happy. He hoped that his fellow Americans would practice neither commerce nor navigation and thus avoid wars.

What he saw in France did not encourage him. Mischief at the top, and misery at the bottom; as he wrote his Italian friend, Professor Bellini:

"I find the general fate of humanity here most deplorable. The truth of Voltaire's observation, offers itself perpetually, that every man here must be either the hammer or the anvil."

He had little patience with the caste-ridden, poverty-stricken world that surrounded him, in spite of its cordial and enthusiastic reception of him.

"Intrigues of love occupy the younger and those of ambition, the elder part of the great. Conjugal love having no existence among them, domestic happiness, of which that is the basis, is utterly unknown."

No American, he believed, should come to Europe under the age of thirty.

"He acquires a fondness for European luxury and dissipation and a contempt for the simplicity of his own country; he is fascinated with the privileges of the European aristocrats, and sees with abhorrence the lovely equality which the poor enjoy with the rich in his own country: . . . he is led by the strongest of all human passions into a spirit for female intrigue destructive of his own and others' happiness, or a passion for whores destructive of his health, and in both cases learns to consider fidelity to the marriage bed as an ungentlemanly practice and inconsistent with happiness: he recollects the voluptuary dress and arts of the European women and pities and despises the chaste affections and simplicity of those of his own country. . . ."

All this he found very much inferior "to the tranquil, permanent felicity with which domestic society in America blesses most of its inhabitants."

He was overcome with the numberless instances of wretchedness on all sides, with the concentration of property in a few hands.

"Of twenty millions of people supposed to be in France I am of opinion there are nineteen millions more wretched, more accursed in every circumstance of human existence than the most conspicuously wretched individual of the whole United States."

But in spite of this he found many of the French polite, self-denying, hospitable, and good-humored, and excelling all others in arts and crafts. Indeed, he wrote to Abigail Adams: "I do love this *people* with all my heart, and think that with a better religion, a better form of government . . . their condition & Country would be most enviable."

As ambassador he had to live in style, although, to be sure, far beyond his means. At the end of his first year he moved to an elegant house at the corner of the Grande Route des Champs Elysées and the rue Neuve de Berry. It had out-buildings, stables, and an extensive garden. He was provided with a carriage and horses, but he could not afford a saddle horse on his income. For exercise, he walked miles each day and, as many Americans have done since, he spent much time savoring the bookstalls. He also kept rooms in the Carthusian monastery on Mount Calvary, to which he could retire whenever the press of business became excessive. Here, with his official papers at hand, he could settle down for a week's uninterrupted work.

He constantly met the most cultivated and distinguished of both sexes and entertained them at his table. He relished France's strawberries, cherries, plums, gooseberries, and pears and found them all better than those in America. And he appreciated its wines and commented in one of his letters that he had never yet seen a man drunk in France. But what he valued and enjoyed most of all was their architecture, sculpture, painting, and music. It was especially for the last of these that he envied them.

If his reports sound gloomy at times for so sanguine a temperament, this tone can be laid partly to the weather. For an American, a Parisian winter can be excessively trying. Jefferson complained of being confined indoors by the extremely damp air. But more than this, he was lonesome, separated as he was from his own country and from his children. During the summer of 1785 he had word from his sister-in-law that his youngest child, little Lucy, had died. He saw Martha at the convent as often as he could, and now he began writing his second daughter, Mary, or Polly, as he called her, urging her to come over to join him: "My dear Polly,

I have not received a letter from you since I came to France. If you knew how much I love you and what pleasure the receipt of your letters gave me at Philadelphia, you would have written me, or at least have told your aunt what to write. . . . I wish so much to see you, that I have desired your uncle and aunt to send you to me. I know, my dear Polly, how sorry you will be, and ought to be, to leave them and your cousins; but your sister and myself cannot live without you. . . ."

And then the usual inducements. She should be taught to play on the harpsichord, to draw, to dance, to read and talk French, so as to be more worthy of the love of her friends. She should also have as many dolls and playthings as she wanted for herself or to send to her cousins. And then her doting Papa added:

"I hope you are a very good girl, that you love your uncle and aunt very much, and are very thankful to them for all their goodness to you; that you never suffer yourself to be angry with any body, that you give your playthings to those who want them, that you do whatever any body desires of you that is right, that you never tell stories, never beg for any thing, mind your books and your work when your aunt tells you, never play but when she permits you, nor go where she forbids you; remember, too, as a constant charge, not to go out without your bonnet, because it will make you very ugly, and then we shall not love you so much. If you always practice these lessons we shall continue to love you as we do now, and it is impossible to love you more."

Her response:

"Dear Papa—

I long to see you, and hope that you and sister Patsy are well; . . . I hope that you will send me a doll. I am very sorry that you have sent for me. I don't want to go to France, I had rather stay with Aunt Eppes.

Your most happy and dutiful daughter,

Polly Jefferson."

Later:

"Dear Papa—

I want to see you and sister Patsy, but you must come to Uncle Eppes's house.

Polly Jefferson."

Man proposes, woman disposes. It was two years before Polly came. She was then a young lady of fifteen years.

Though Jefferson did not often reveal his deeper feelings, in September 1785, one year after he had come to Paris, he wrote a letter to his friend James Currie which shows how homesick and hungry for news he must have been:

"Of political correspondents I can find enough, but I can persuade nobody to believe that the small facts which they see daily under their eyes are precious to me at this distance; much more interesting to the heart than events of higher rank. Fancy to yourself a being who is withdrawn from his connections of blood, of marriage, of friendship, of acquaintance in all their gradations, who for years should hear nothing of what has passed among them, who returns again to see them and finds the one-half dead. This strikes him like a pestilence sweeping off the half of mankind. Events which had they come to him one by one and in detail he would have weathered as other people do, when presented to his mind all at once are overwhelming. Continue then to give me facts, little facts, such as you think every one imagines beneath notice, and your letters will be the most precious to me. They will place me in imagination in my own country, and they will place me where I am happiest."

But where was he now happiest? At home, with the constant and poignant reminders of his loss? Or in the sophisticated salons of Paris, with their worldliness? Or in the simple French country-side, where he could relish the landscape and the ways of the peasants? It was the last of these that seemed to give him the greatest satisfaction.

CHAPTER NINE

❧ 9 ❧

Toward the end of February 1786, Colonel William Stephens Smith, John Adams's future son-in-law, who was secretary of the legation in London, arrived in Paris with a letter from his chief, urging Jefferson to come at once to London to enter into negotiations with the Portuguese ambassador. Jefferson left Paris on March 6 and reached London five days later. It soon became apparent to him that the piratical powers of the Barbary States were aiming to extort tribute to the tune of some $660,000. Congress had authorized no such expenditures. When the American commissioner tactfully demanded to know on what ground these depredations were being made on nations which had done them no injury, he was told, in effect, that it was written in the Koran that all nations which had not acknowledged the Prophet were sinners and that it was the right and duty of the faithful to plunder and enslave them.

Jefferson thereupon confined his efforts to the deliverance of captives by ransom. Indeed, he continued these efforts during the remainder of his residence in Paris and long after his return home. He had to keep strictly secret the fact that his government had authorized him to treat for the release of the captives. Had this fact leaked out, the price of their ransom would have skyrocketed. Jefferson naturally came in for much censure from the captives for appearing to have disobeyed the orders of Congress, whereas actually he was continuing his efforts to free them until as late as 1793. As in other instances in his life, he said not a word in self-defense.

Adams and Jefferson now addressed themselves to a commercial treaty to be offered to England. They were not too sanguine about its outcome, since they were both being given the cold shoulder.

"On my presentation, as usual, to the King and Queen at their levées, it was impossible for anything to be more ungracious, than their notice of Mr. Adams and myself. I saw, at once, that the ulcerations of the mind in that mulish being left nothing to be expected on the subject of my attendance."

So wrote Jefferson, who felt, perhaps more than Adams, the chill and rude reception at the hands of the sovereign whose tyrannical temper had been so sharply attacked by Jefferson's gifted pen. Adams was conscious of the guilt and shame in the faces of the English when they looked at him, but to George III he was willing to grant some virtues as an accomplished courtier, despite the king's full and sullen obstinacy. He wrote to John Jay on December 15, 1785: "So much of his [the king's] time is, and has been consumed in this [small talk] that he is in all the great affairs of society and government as *weak,* as far as I can judge, as we ever understood him to be in America. He is also *obstinate. . . .*"

Jefferson was quite well aware of how much the British hated the new nation—even more than during the war, though they recognized the importance of a trade relationship with America. In the comfortable companionship of the Adamses, he took flight from the painful derision to which he was exposed. Abigail's great admiration of him was soothing, and her lively and inquisitive mind he found greatly entertaining, while John, if peppery, and fundamentally anti-French in his bias, was experienced and wise and on the whole tougher and less sensitive than his Virginian friend. As was his custom, Jefferson made the most of his opportunities by seeing all he could of the countryside. He kept a brief journal, principally confined to gardens and gardening. He mentions, among many others well known to a contemporary

American traveler, Chiswick, Hampton Court, Stowe, Blenheim, and Kew. His comments are on the whole dry and practical rather than aesthetic, for he was concerned with measurements, with the height and width of things and their cost. One of his biographers says of him that he looked, even at the beautiful, with a sort of "arithmetical eye."

On his return to France after two months' absence, Jefferson wrote his general impressions of England to his old friend Page. Comparing it with France, he found a much greater proportion of barren land, not better cultivated, but better manured and therefore more productive. But he owned readily that the pleasure of gardening in England was "the article in which it surpasses all the earth," far beyond his expectation. Then he added: "The city of London, though handsomer than Paris, is not so handsome as Philadelphia. Their architecture is in the most wretched style I ever saw, not meaning to except America, where it is bad, nor even Virginia, where it is worse than in any other part of America which I have seen."

One cannot escape the impression that Jefferson's eye was influenced by his anti-British feelings and that these caused him to withhold the usual spontaneous enthusiasm of any cultivated tourist. His journal does not even mention that on April 6 he left Banbury Cross by post-chaise for Stratford-upon-Avon.* Although Jefferson held the writings of Shakespeare in highest esteem, the one reference to him is in the account-book, which says dryly, "paid postillion 3s.; for seeing house where Shakespeare was born, 1s.; seeing his tombstone, 1s.; entertainment, 4s. 2d.; servants 2s.; horses to Hackley, 12s." There is no other mention of the Bard; nor of the sacred memorials of Westminster Abbey; nor of the classic precincts of Oxford.

That he recorded nothing does not mean he felt nothing. As in his affectional life, so also in his aesthetic, he was inclined to taciturnity. But his relations with his children and his close associates show him to have been a man of deep sentiment, even warmth, though always reserved and controlled. And his house and

* This writer recalls traveling on foot in his youth over the same road, to his great delight.

grounds and gardens speak for his taste and his love of the beautiful more than any sentimental or poetical outbursts could have done. His vivid feelings show themselves in his responses to France and above all to Lafayette, for whom he entertained the greatest respect and attachment. Indeed, Lafayette symbolized for Jefferson the best of that nation. Jefferson wrote:

"If anybody thinks that kings, nobles, or priests are good conservators of the public happiness, send him here. . . . The omnipotence of their effect cannot be better proved, than in this country, particularly, where, notwithstanding the finest soil upon earth, the finest climate under heaven, and a people often most benevolent, the most gay and amiable character of which the human form is susceptible; where such a people, I say, surrounded by so many blessings from nature, are loaded with misery, by kings, nobles, and priests, and by them alone."

He believed that only the people can protect themselves against these evils and that the tax paid for this purpose is not more than a thousandth part of the cost of supporting a monarchy or a hierarchy of nobles and clerics. Jefferson was, and always remained, an ardent and constant democrat.

As a gesture of his devotion to France, he presented to the city of Paris, on behalf of the Commonwealth of Virginia, a bust of Lafayette. It was accepted at an appropriate exercise in the Hôtel de Ville, where he thought it would most honor the subject and at the same time gratify the feelings of an allied nation. Unfortunately, he could not be present in person at the time of presentation because of an accident.

Shortly before, Jefferson had met with an unfortunate mishap. In his methodical way, his habit was to ride out or walk in the country every afternoon, often as far as seven miles. On September 4, 1786, while in France, returning from one of these rambles in the company of a friend and while engaged in earnest conversation, he slipped and fell and dislocated or fractured his right wrist. He said nothing to his companion of the painful accident, but grasped the injured arm in his other hand and held it behind his back. He was four or five miles from his residence when this accident occurred. Continuing his conversation without betraying the slightest evidence of the intense pain he was suffering, he finally sent for a surgeon. But by the time the surgeon came, the arm was so swollen that the fracture could not be set, and the arm remained weak and stiff forever after.

This version of the accident is based on a description written by his daughter Martha and published by his biographer, Henry S. Randall. The same account is provided by Parton, who mentions also that, on the very afternoon of the accident, Jefferson entered into his account book with *his left hand* the fact that he had given 24 f. 10 c. for buttons and 4 f. 6 c. for gloves and the next day he paid 3 f. to see the king's library. Three days later, according to Randall, he went to see the château at Marly and the water works that pump water into the fountains at Versailles. All this would have been consistent with a certain stoicism in him. But there is another version of the story, which shows him in a different light.

According to this one, the damage to his wrist occurred not on September 4, but a fortnight later. Dr. Lyman H. Butterfield, distinguished historical editor, deserves the credit for setting the matter straight. It may seem but a pedantic point; and yet it proves to be not so, for it shows a side of Jefferson which he usually managed to keep hidden. The evidence suggests that he fell and hurt his wrist some time between September 14 and 22, probably on the eighteenth, when he "pd. two Surgeons 12 F."

He had been spending many a delightful afternoon driving through the western suburbs of Paris, and he had visited such showplaces as the Forest of Marly and the nearby Désert de Retz. He was not alone on these sightseeing expeditions, nor yet with an unnamed male companion as his daughter had suggested in her note, but with a bewitching, coquettish, and gifted lady of twenty-seven. Maria Cosway was of an English family, though born in Italy, where she had studied art and music. Herself an artist, she was married to Richard Cosway, a well-known miniaturist, considerably older than herself. What more natural than that Jefferson, a lonely and now middle-aged widower, should have lost his heart and almost his head to this lovely and attractive, though perhaps self-centered, young woman with whom he shared so many aesthetic and intellectual delights? At any rate, her husband was busy painting portraits and seeing prospective clients, and had left his wife pretty much to her own devices. He was from all accounts an unattractive, monkey-faced little man whom Maria had married partly out of convenience to replenish the dwindling family fortune after her father's death in Italy.

Jefferson had met the Cosways through his friend, the American artist John Trumbull. He was at once struck with Maria's beauty, crowned, as it was, "with a mass of curly golden hair." He soon learned that she not only painted but had many musical accomplishments as well. She sang, played the harp and the pianoforte, and composed songs. Furthermore, she spoke a mixture of languages in a deliciously soft voice, alluring yet comforting. The austere Jefferson was quite bowled over; he spent as much time with her as he could, even at the expense of his official duties. This was not like him. Though punctilious about always conveying his respects to Mr. Cosway in his messages to her, there is more than a hint of the clandestine in the meetings he arranged. She encouraged him and was excitingly flirtatious—obviously flattered by the serious attentions of this tall, distinguished-looking foreigner with whom she shared so many tastes and interests. From her self-portrait one cannot escape the impression of a vain, self-centered young thing, a baby-doll with a small, ungenerous rosebud mouth, the kind of young woman that a serious-minded, middle-aged widower might easily fall for. And fall he did, figuratively as well as literally.

On one of their happy outings, while promenading in the Cours la Reine, along the Seine from the Place de la Concorde, Jefferson must have been feeling his oats, for in spite of his mature years—he was then forty-three—he jumped over a low fence, caught his foot, and crashed to the ground. He tried to break the fall with his right hand, but succeeded only in breaking or dislocating his wrist. Without benefit of X-rays, it would be impossible to say which. Whatever the nature of the injury, it caused him agonizing pain and confined him to his residence for a couple of weeks. During this time his secretary wrote all his letters for him.

About two weeks after the accident, he managed a shaky letter to Maria, written with his left hand. She replied promptly. Her letter, though coquettish, was full of sympathy.

After a sleepless night, he impetuously decided that he must see her, since she was leaving immediately for England. He accompanied the Cosways to the post house at St. Denis, where he helped his lady love into her carriage, turning "more dead than alive" (his words) to his own, to be driven home.

Even at the time of this accident, which perforce changed his immediate plans, Jefferson seems to have been aware of its deeper meaning for him. Perhaps because he was confined to his rooms for some weeks, he felt it as the passing of his youth and the beginning of middle age. This comes with the force of revelation to some men. He was now over the watershed of his life. He would never again allow his heart to prevail over his head—not because of guilt or hurt, but because, for him, his head was the more trustworthy instrument. In spite of his strong, romantic nature, he was a realist, and his reality lay in other directions.

Three weeks after the accident he wrote his friend William S. Smith: "How the right hand became disabled would be a long story for the left to tell. It was by one of those follies from which good cannot come, but ill may." This cryptic remark could have dropped from the lips of one of Macbeth's witches. Jefferson was, of course, referring to the difficulty of writing with his left hand and to the folly of a man of his dignity and habits kicking up his heels and vaulting a barrier. But this was not his only folly. The other folly from which, as he said, "good cannot come but ill may" was the folly of giving way to his emotions, represented here as in a dream by his left hand, whereas the intellect and rational control is represented by the right. He knew that it was dangerous for a man approaching middle age, who had always held himself in check, to give way to his erotic emotions. The way back may be hard to find.

Jefferson's sudden and passionate love for this irresistible child-woman is a familiar enough story. C. G. Jung called such a woman an *anima* figure—a symbol of the eternal female in which men see reflected their own unconscious femininity to which they are desperately attracted. Jefferson was certainly enthralled by his *belle dame,* perhaps especially so because her many gifts appealed to his head as well as to his heart. His well-known dialogue between his head and his heart addressed to Maria exposes this conflict. Though written in the form of a letter to her, it is really a soliloquy—in which the two sides of Jefferson converse with each other. The "Heart" speaks for the tender-feeling, emotional female side of the writer, while the "Head" is the voice of his practical, rational, and controlled male side. They are for the moment at loggerheads. This letter was written with obvious difficulty with Mr. Jefferson's left hand, indicating how urgently he felt the need to write it. When printed, it covers some twelve pages.

It has been called "one of the most unusual tributes ever paid a pretty woman by a distinguished man." Perhaps so, from one point of view, but from another one can see it as the effort of a sorely troubled man to come to peace with himself and his turbulent feelings. Here are some brief, random excerpts from the document. His Heart says: "I am indeed the most wretched of earthly beings. Overwhelmed with grief. . . . I would willingly meet whatever catastrophe should leave me no more to feel, or to fear." His Head then chides him and tells him that these feelings are "the eternal consequences of your warmth and precipitation" and that it is imprudent to place one's affections without reserve on objects one must soon lose and whose loss must cause such severe pangs. Then the Head continues: "Do not bite at the bait of pleasure, till you know there is no hook beneath it. . . . The art of life is the art of avoiding pain. . . . The most effectual means of being secure against pain; is to retire within ourselves, and to suffice for our own happiness. Those which depend on ourselves, are the only pleasures a wise man will count on; for nothing is ours, which another may deprive us of. Hence the inestimable value of intellectual pleasures. . . . Friendship is but another name for an alliance with the follies and the misfortunes of others. . . ." But the Heart counters with: "And what more sublime delight than to mingle tears with one whom the hand of heaven hath smitten! . . . Deeply practised in the school of affliction, the human heart knows no joy which I have not lost, no sorrow of which I have not drunk! Fortune can present no grief of unknown form to me."

And so the antiphonal, not to say ambivalent, song goes. To the modern reader it seems curiously baroque and contorted and self-pitying. Men no longer try to win ladies' hearts by playing the "merryman moping mum," nor by showing them how deeply practiced they are in the school of affliction, nor yet by being insufferably and boringly rational. Perhaps time and experience and the pragmatic temper in which we live have taught us that neither method suffices. But Jefferson was a child of his times, as we are of ours, and in the eighteenth century such divagations were quite acceptable.

In any event, the affair of the heart gradually changed into a tender friendship, with little opportunity for seeing each other. Jefferson hoped to persuade his Maria to come to America and behold with her own eyes the glories of Virginia; "the Falling Spring, the Cascade of Niagara, the Passage of the Powtowmac through the Blue Mountains, the Natural Bridge . . . and our own dear Monticello, where has nature spread so rich a mantle under the eye?"

But she never came.

CHAPTER TEN

❦

On December 14, 1786, Jefferson wrote his sister-in-law, Mrs. Eppes, "An unfortunate dislocation of my right wrist has disabled me from writing for three months. I have as yet no use of it, except that I can write a little, but slowly and in great pain." He did not mention that he never again would be able to play his beloved fiddle, which must have been a sore deprivation for him. In a few days he was to set out for the south of France, "to try the effect of some mineral waters there." It may seem strange that a man as scientifically sophisticated as Jefferson was in medical matters, as in others, should have expected any benefit for a dislocated or broken wrist from drinking the mineral waters at Aix-en-Provence. But this faith was kept alive by that credulous though not wholly disinterested breed of spa doctors.

Whether the waters did him good or not, the new sights and beauties he saw in his travels were balm to his spirit. From Nîmes he wrote on March 20, 1787, to his friend the Comtesse de Tesse, an aunt of Madame Lafayette: "Here I am, Madam, gazing whole hours at the Maison Quarrée, like a lover at his mistress. . . . This is the second time I have been in love since I left Paris. The first was with a Diana at the Chateau de Laye-Epinaye in Beaujolais, a delicious morsel of sculpture. . . ." And he was violently smitten (his words) with the Hôtel de Salm at the Tuileries, where he went almost daily, just to look.

He spent little time in the great cities; in fact, as he wrote Lafayette, he "gulped" each down in a day, but over the olive groves and the orangeries he was in raptures. He urged Lafayette to travel incognito so that he could get to know his own country—"ferret the people out of their hovels, as I have done, look into their kettles, eat their bread, loll on their beds under pretense of resting yourself, but in fact to find out if they are soft." He promised him great reward if he would apply the knowledge thus gained to improving the lot of the common people.

The journal of Jefferson's travels in France is occupied chiefly, as it was in England, with practical descriptions, but in place of gardening it is more concerned with wine-making and agriculture. His information is detailed and extensive and often exact enough to enable a neophyte to take up viniculture. Jefferson traveled alone in his own carriage, with post horses. He had left Martha at the convent school in Panthemont in Paris. His route lay up the Seine, through Champagne and Burgundy, and then down the Saône and the Rhône through Beaujolais, Dauphiné, Orange, and Languedoc to Aix. Although he spent four days at Lyon, he dismissed the city in as many lines; but he examined with meticulous care the Roman remains at Nîmes, including the amphitheater and the temple and fountain of Diana. He had previously obtained the plan of the Maison Quarrée and sent it to Virginia as a model for its capitol. Of Virginia architecture he had little good to say: on the contrary, he believed that its "genius . . .. seems to have shed its maledictions over this land."

But he was not one for negative complaints. He had made plans for redesigning the palace and the college in Williamsburg; and when he was only twenty-four he had begun the design of Monticello, where he said all his wishes ended, as he hoped his days would. Jefferson was a disciple of the great sixteenth-century Italian architect Palladio, who became the ultimate authority for him. His idea of placing his classical villa on a mountaintop may have derived from Palladio, as indeed did many of his other architectural plans, but no doubt he was influenced by the enchanting views offered by the elevation on which it stood.

In later years he was to write, "Architecture is my delight, and putting up, and pulling down, one of my favorite amusements." He designed and planned changes in every house he ever lived in, from Monticello to his residence on the Champs Elysées to the White House. Indeed, he helped L'Enfant with ideas for his design of Washington, lending him town plans of many European cities. Later in life he was responsible for redesigning Pennsylvania Avenue, dividing it by rows of trees to separate the road from the sidewalks. But, above all, and even when burdened with the presidency, Jefferson found time to be occupied with Monticello. In 1796, after eight years of war and another ten of absence, he wrote that his house had gone into almost total decay, but he set to work at repairing it.

But to continue with his journey—three days after Jefferson reached Aix on March 25, 1787, he wrote a long letter to his daughter Martha, in which he imparted much of his philosophy of life. He began by telling her that he hoped the mineral waters of Aix might restore strength to his wrists, but that other considerations had a share in inducing him to undertake his journey; and he mentioned instruction, amusement, and abstraction from business, of which he had had too much at Paris. Naturally, he did not mention the emotional storm he himself had just been through. He urged her to cultivate habits of industry and activity, saying:

"Of all the cankers of human happiness, none corrodes with so silent, yet so baneful a tooth, as indolence. . . . Idleness begets ennui, ennui the hypochondria, and that a diseased body. No laborious person was ever yet hysterical. . . . If at any moment, my dear, you catch yourself in idleness, start from it as you would from the precipice of a gulf. . . . My expectations from you are high—yet not higher than you may attain. Industry and resolution are all that you are wanting. Nobody in this world can make me so happy, or so miserable, as you. Retirement from public life will ere long be necessary for me. To your sister and yourself I look to render the evening of my life serene and contented. Its morning has been clouded by loss after loss, till I have nothing left but you. I do not doubt either your affection or dispositions. But great exertions are necessary, and you have little time left to make them. Be industrious, then, my dear child. Think nothing unsurmountable by resolution and application, and you will be all I wish you to be."

When she complained that the Italian translation of Livy which her father had given her put her out of her wits, he wrote:

"I do not like your saying that you are unable to read the antient print of your Livy but with the aid of your master. We are always equal to what we undertake with resolution. . . . It is part of the American character to consider nothing as desperate; to surmount every difficulty by resolution and contrivance. . . . Consider therefore the conquering your Livy as an exercise in the habit of surmounting difficulties, a habit which will be necessary to you in the country where you are to live. . . ."

Martha was still only a girl of fifteen. Fortunately, she was of a sanguine, loving, and enthusiastic disposition; and instead of rejecting her father's sententious, somber, and worrisome advice she took it to heart and patterned herself after him. The fact that he was so loving and so constantly kind no doubt softened the effect of his moralizing. There are other letters to Martha from this period, dated at Toulon, Marseilles, Nantes, and again at Paris, which he reached on June 10, after an absence of some six months. Apparently Jefferson soon became convinced that the waters of Aix were doing him no good, so he cut short his stay. He then proceeded on his travels as indicated in his letters, which to his elder daughter are all signed: "Yours affectionately, Th. Jefferson." She had written him: "I hope your wrist is better, and I am inclined to think that your voyage is rather for your pleasure than your health; however, I hope it will answer both purposes." From Toulon he instructed her on how to behave toward her younger sister, Polly, when she arrived during the summer.

"Teach her above all things to be good—because without that, we can neither be valued by others, nor set any value on ourselves. Teach her, to be always true; no vice is so mean as the want of truth, and at the same time so useless. Teach her never to be angry. Anger only serves to torment ourselves, to divert others, and alienate their esteem. And teach her industry and application to useful pursuits." If you teach her these things, he argued, you will be more fixed in them yourself and you will increase "the happiness of him who loves you infinitely. . . ."

From Nice, on his forty-fourth birthday, Jefferson crossed the Alps on muleback, the snows being still too deep to permit the passage of carriages. In Turin he examined samples of Piedmont rice, which was cleaned by the same type of machines that were used in Carolina, but apparently Carolina rice broke in the process. He finally concluded that the superiority of European rice was inherent in the species. He described the rice-beaters in great detail.

"They are eight feet nine inches long. Their ends, instead of being a truncated cone, have nine teeth of iron, bound closely together. Each tooth is a double pyramid, joined at the base. When put together, they stand with the upper ends placed in contact, so as to form them into one great cone, and the lower ends diverging. The upper are socketed into the end of the pestle," etc., etc. And so he went on, always writing out his specifications in his meticulous way, as if for a machine shop.

Jefferson soon learned that exportation of rough rice from this region of Italy was punishable by death. Even so, he crammed his coat pockets full of it and hired a muleteer to take a couple of sacks of it across the Apennines to Genoa, with the hope of sending the seed to the rice-producing states in America. In all his travels and explorations, he always had his own country in mind first and how his observations could benefit it. To his friend Wythe he wrote that he was persuaded that there were "many parts of our lower country where the olive tree might be raised, which is assuredly the richest gift of heaven. I can scarcely except bread. I see this tree supporting thousands among the Alps, where there is not soil enough to make bread for a single family."

He was always the questing, questioning tourist, with no time to waste, not even time enough to visit Venice or Florence or Rome. It has been said of him that "a steam wheel excited him more than a Titian and that he would travel farther to see a new machine than an old Michelangelo." It may well astound us that even the engineering genius of Leonardo seems to have passed him by; at any rate, he did not go to Florence.

On May 21 he again wrote Martha, this time from the canal at Languedoc, on whose limpid waters, under cloudless skies, he had been sailing for a week, with a row of nightingales in full chorus on each side of him. He urged her to make herself "acquainted with the music of this bird," so that when she returned to her own country she might compare it to the mockingbird, which has the advantage of singing throughout a great part of the year, whereas the nightingale sings for only five or six weeks in the spring and for a still shorter time and with a more feeble voice in the fall. Again he reminded her of "the true secret, the grand recipe, for felicity"—to be always employed. "The idle are the only wretched." In his next letter, written after his return to Paris, he told her to hurry making her gown and her redingote, because she would be going with him "some day next week to dine at the Marquis Fayette's."

To Madison he wrote the next month, declaring that he was happy over the re-entry of Malesherbes into the king's council, because with him he had established the most unreserved intimacy. He was also pleased with Montmorin, he said, whose honesty proceeded from his heart as well as from his head and therefore might be more surely counted on. The king was described as loving business, economy, order, and justice and sincerely wishing for the good of his people. But, according to Jefferson, he was irascible, rude, and limited in his understanding and in religious matters. He was, Jefferson said, too fond of the pleasures of the table, and his propensity for drink had recently increased. He bordered on bigotry. He had no mistress, loved his queen, and was too much governed by her; and she, in turn, was capricious, devoted to pleasure and expense, and not remarkable for any other vices or virtues.

In July, Jefferson's second daughter, Mary, reached London. She had reluctantly and tearfully parted from her aunt and uncle and their children and, in the charge of a young Negro servant girl, had crossed the ocean to be received in England by Mrs. Adams. Impatient of Mary's arrival in France, but too much occupied to go himself, Jefferson sent his steward, Petit, after her. Maria, as she was soon to be called—perhaps in honor of Maria

Cosway—reached her father's hotel on the twenty-ninth of July, three days before her ninth birthday. She soon joined Martha at the convent school.

Mrs. Adams was ecstatic in her praise of the child. She wrote to her sister, saying that a finer child of her age she had never seen, so mature and womanly and of so much sensibility. "She clung round me so that I could not help shedding a tear at parting with her. She was the favorite of every one in the house. I regret that such fine spirits must be spent in the walls of a convent. She is a beautiful girl, too."

Jefferson was now content; he had his two jewels with him. A most unusual relationship existed between him and his daughters. He enveloped them in a kind of motherly softness. And yet he was firm, calm, and always just. He was never angry or even impatient with them. No need of theirs was too small to be attended to; he insisted on buying them all their clothes. Is there any wonder that they and their children adored and venerated him, as each in turn attested? They seem not to have been intimidated by him, for he was unfailingly kind.

Jefferson had the reputation for being cold and withdrawn. His natural reserve and his superior gifts may have seemed intimidating. He was more at ease with the young than with adults—not only his children and grandchildren, but many young men turned to him naturally for advice and guidance about their educations. These included both Jack Eppes and Thomas Mann Randolph, before Jefferson had any idea that they would marry his daughters; also young John Rutledge, the son of the statesman of that name, of South Carolina; and Thomas Lee Shippen, whose father was Dr. William Shippen of Philadelphia. Toward William Short, his young secretary, he felt and behaved like a wise father to a devoted son.

There were many adoring women who added to the charm and gaiety of his circle. Among them were Maria Cosway, whom we have already mentioned, and her friend Angelica Church, the sister-in-law of Alexander Hamilton, "two little women," as Angelica wrote Jefferson, "who are extremely vain of the pleasure of being permitted to write him, and very happy to have some share

of his favorable opinion." Toward them Jefferson combined the
gallantry of an eighteenth-century courtier with the warmth and
affection of a sincere friend. He had a special relationship with
Madame de Corny, whose husband was a liberal-minded friend of
Lafayette and of America. She is described as lovely, delicate and
essentially feminine, and much flattered by the friendship of this
great man. He carried on an active correspondence and conversations with Lafayette's aunt, Madame de Tesse, with whom he exchanged views on gardens and architecture. To her, Jefferson was
the apostle of republicanism, and at her house he met Madame de
Tott, with whom he read Homer. In recounting his many and diversified friends, one may not omit John and Abigail Adams, who
perhaps headed the list, and the painter John Trumbull, who
had a standing invitation to occupy a bed at the Hôtel de Lan-
geac. Trumbull painted likenesses of many famous patriots, including General and Mrs. Washington, Alexander Hamilton,
John Jay, and Timothy Dwight, the president of Yale. He also
painted, in Benjamin West's studio in London, *The Battle of
Bunker Hill, The Death of Montgomery*, and later, on his return
to America, *The Signing of the Declaration of Independence*.
Through Trumbull, Jefferson commissioned Mather Brown to do
a portrait of Thomas Paine. Brown did one of Jefferson, as well,
representing him as a man of fashion, which he was not, with his
hair powdered and rolled over his ears, and long, gracile, feminine
fingers, and wearing an expression at once earnest, shrewd, and
triste. But Trumbull's portrait of Jefferson, done in Paris, shows
him with a stronger, more vigorous face and unpowdered hair,
and is probably more in character.

In the spring of 1788 Jefferson traveled to Holland and Germany. At The Hague he greeted John Adams, the American minister to France, and conferred with him on diplomatic business.
He then went to Amsterdam, Utrecht, and Nimwegen. The mechanical ingenuity of the Dutch impressed him greatly and he
made sketches of the details of house construction and furnishings
—even such household objects as oil and vinegar cruets, hexago-
nal lanterns, the marks on porcelain. Crossing over into Germany,
he was oppressed, as many travelers have been since, by what he

saw. "The soil and climate are the same," he observed; "the governments alone differ." He thought that he saw a servile fear in the faces of the Prussian subjects, who lived in an atmosphere of universal and equal poverty in thatch-covered mud houses. But he admired the hogs of Westphalia, and the Moselle wines in the region of Coblenz. Here he saw an invention which would become familiar enough in America. In the Elector's palace the rooms were heated "by warm air conveyed from an oven below, through tubes which open into the rooms." Frankfort was a free city, independent, rich, and active, and by contrast Hanau was a ghost town. Jefferson put it this way:

"In Frankfort all is life, bustle and motion; in Hanau the silence and quiet of the mansions of the dead. Nobody is seen moving in the streets; every door is shut; no sound of the saw, the hammer, or other utensil of industry. The drum and fife is all that is heard."

Toward the end of April, after a journey of about seven weeks, he was back in Paris, where he rejoined his loving daughters. In many ways they fulfilled his life and gave him the opportunity of mothering them which afforded a good outlet to this female side of his nature. Perhaps a well-tempered mind such as Jefferson possessed occurs only in people who exhibit just this mixture of active-passive, masculine-feminine components.

CHAPTER ELEVEN

❦

Back in Paris Jefferson resumed his ministerial duties, after three and a half months which had passed more delightfully than any he had ever experienced. On his travels, he had searched out whatever awakened his interest or fed his insatiable curiosity, always with an eye to what would benefit his own country, which he looked upon with undeviating devotion as a kind of idealized fellow human. Everything was grist for his mill, and so he either described or sketched such objects as bridges, the joists of houses, window sills, brick arches, flagstaffs, dining tables with removable leaves, curtained bedsteads with iron rods, flues of stoves, a machine for drawing empty boats over a dam, wind sawmills, wheelbarrows, hooks for holding up vines, and moldboards. In fact, the moldboard plow was his brain child. Its perfection, he said, depended on mathematical principles, and therefore it could be made by the most bungling carpenter. It consisted of "two wedges combined at right angles, the first in the direct line of the furrow to raise the turf gradually, the other across the furrow to turn it over gradually."

In the journal of his travels, there is scarcely mention of another human being or of a personal encounter. He seemed content to be alone as long as he had new sights and sounds to engage him. But in Paris he turned to other matters. Two in particular commanded his attention, one on his side of the ocean and the other across it in America. The first was the Assembly of Notables at Versailles, whom Louis XVI had charged with keeping him informed about the rapidly deteriorating state of the French nation; and the second was the Constitutional Convention, at that time sitting in Philadelphia. Distance prevented Jefferson from taking an active part in the affairs at home, and his diplomatic status kept him from interfering with French policy or politics. But he had his own way of exerting his influence, either by correspondence or by word of mouth to chosen and strategically placed persons.

In France, Jefferson cautioned his friend the Marquis de Lafayette against aping the young American nation, urging him instead to proceed not by revolution but gradually, as England had done, in approaching a good constitution. France, after all, had been a monarchy for over a thousand years; and Jefferson, in spite of his hatred of monarchs, was wise enough to see that France could not suddenly and with safety break with the past. Instead of overcoming the king by force, Jefferson advised buying him off and filling the royal coffers with gold. Still, he could sense the coming events in the turbulent air. In March 1789, he wrote to his artist friend Madame de Bréhan, "A great political revolution will take place in your country, and that without bloodshed." His own aloof, gentle high-mindedness and his natural identification with the liberal French aristocrats prevented him from recognizing the surging power of the Third Estate of artisans, the bourgeoisie, and the lower clergy. Taxation weighed heavily on these, while the financial administration was one of disorder, corruption, and misrule. The government was sinking in a mire of bankruptcy.

The winter of 1789 had been a bitter one, with floods and hailstorms destroying half the harvest and leading to general unemployment, misery, and widespread fear of starvation. Louis XVI then assembled the Estates General, the national legislative body, with representation, unlike the English Parliament, by Estates. But the Third Estate was intransigent and defiant. It seceded from the Estates General and set itself up as the National Assembly. Several of the Deputies had met at Jefferson's house for his counsel and guidance. He was far too wise and diplomatically prudent to give advice against the king, but his association with this liberal group of patriots kept him informed of the views and intentions of the revolutionary party. He was no extremist and continued to urge the avoidance of violence. He advised compromising with the king. But history moved at its own pace. Tempers in Paris and at Versailles were at the boiling point. On the fateful day of July 14, the angry crowd stormed the Bastille and killed its governor.

A week later the chairman of the newly formed French Constitutional Committee addressed a letter to Jefferson, begging for an interview, "being anxious not to neglect anything in order to bring to perfection so important an undertaking." Jefferson, with great politeness, begged off on the grounds of his being a stranger. But the committee members, under the leadership of Lafayette, met at the American's for dinner. Eight of them sat around his table from four in the afternoon till ten at night, Jefferson as a "silent witness" to their debate, which he thought worthy of "the finest dialogues of antiquity." His calm dignity, self-control, and reasonableness all served to put a check on the Frenchmen's tempers and to help the delegates find agreement among themselves. This was his principal and last contribution to the French Revolution.

At home, the Constitutional Convention was sitting in Philadelphia. Jefferson, as the author of the Declaration of Independence, should have been one of its leading members and would have been had he not been separated by three thousand miles of ocean. He did what he could through his letters to impress his point of view on his compatriots. But letters involved a delay in his communications from several weeks to several months, depending upon wind and weather. He was, however, a tireless and persuasive correspondent. He wrote to James Madison; to George Wythe; to Edward Rutledge, the governor of South Carolina; to George Mason; and to Washington. Madison had sent Jefferson a copy of the Constitution, and to him Jefferson wrote his most penetrating and critical letters. Madison was only eight years Jefferson's junior but felt toward him as a son to a kind and wise father. A storm in Massachusetts known as Shays' Rebellion—an uprising of farmers and debtors—had disturbed Jefferson's equanimity, but less so than it had Madison's or Washington's or even Adams's. Jefferson was all for pardoning the rebels. On February 22, 1787, he had written Mrs. Adams: "The spirit of resistance to government is so valuable on certain occasions, that I wish it to be always kept alive. It will often be exercised when wrong, but better so than not to be exercised at all. I like a little rebellion now and then. It is like a storm in the atmosphere." Perhaps he liked rebellion more than he feared authoritarian repression, of which he had seen too much in Europe. He was persuaded that the good sense of the people was the best army: even if they go wrong for a while, in the long run they will soon correct themselves. He never doubted that the opinion of the people was the proper basis of government. And most important for the progress and security of society was the dissemination of knowledge. Nor did he really question the virtue and superiority of a republican form of government. "But with all the imperfections of our present government, it is without comparison the best existing or that ever did exist." He compared the government of the United States with Europe in terms of heaven and hell— England, like the earth, occupying an intermediate station. The Confederation he regarded as a wonderfully perfect instrument, especially if one considered the circumstances under which it was formed. But it was by no means all to his liking. He approved the division of government into legislative, judiciary, and executive branches; he approved the provision that gave the legislature the powers to levy taxes; he liked the idea that the big states and the little ones have equal representation in the Senate; and he liked the veto power granted the president. But in the original draft Jefferson objected that human rights and civil liberties were not properly safeguarded. He objected as well to "the omission of a bill of rights providing clearly, & without the aid of sophisms for the freedom of religion, freedom of the press, protection against standing armies, restriction against monopolies, the eternal & unremitting force of the habeas corpus laws, and trials by jury in all matters of fact triable by the laws of the land and not by the laws of nations." He added that "a bill of rights is what the people are entitled to against every government on earth . . . & what no just government should refuse." This measure alone would have ensured his fame.

Another feature of the Constitution to which he took exception was that no proper provision had been made for the rotation of the presidency. He felt sure that "the first magistrate will always be re-elected if the Constitution permits it." The notion of a president for life ran counter to all his cherished republican principles. He was willing to trust the farmers of the country, but he had serious misgivings about industrial workers and slum-dwellers, who must be wrong-headed to prefer the filth of crowded cities to the clean air and open spaces of the country. His final view of the Constitution after a Bill of Rights had been added was that it was "unquestionably the wisest ever yet presented to men." That his many suggestions and emendations were adopted and built into the Constitution was a source of deep gratification to him.

Jefferson now felt that his work in Europe was finished. France had become a prison to him, he said. Finally he obtained the president's consent to return to America for a visit, thinking that he would surely go back to his post in a few months. But this was not to be.

Some time before, he had removed his daughters from their convent school, because Martha had expressed the wish to enter a convent. He called for the girls and whisked them away without ever mentioning the subject to his elder daughter, nor she to him. This kind of impetuosity was by no means characteristic of him, but it represented a cherished view of religious freedom with which he could not compromise.

Many years later, he paid tribute, in his *Autobiography,* to the country that had been his home for five years.

". . . I cannot leave this great and good country without expressing my sense of its preeminence of character among the nations of the earth. A more benevolent people, I have never known, nor greater warmth & devotedness in their select friendships. Their kindness and accommodation to strangers is unparalleled, and the hospitality of Paris beyond anything I had conceived to be practicable in a large city. Their eminence too in science, the communicative dispositions of their scientific men, the politeness of the general manners, the ease and vivacity of their conversation, give a charm to their society to be found no where else."

He added that he would of course rather live at home among his friends and relations and the happy recollections of his youth, but that his second choice would always be France.

On October 8, 1789, Jefferson left France, accompanied by his two daughters. After waiting two weeks for favorable winds, they set sail from Yarmouth and reached Norfolk, Virginia, after a smooth passage of one month's duration. This closed a most important chapter in Jefferson's life. He was never to return to France.

CHAPTER TWELVE

❧ ❦

Their voyage home, according to Martha, was quick and not unpleasant. Through Colonel Trumbull's influence, Mr. Pitt, the English Prime Minister, arranged to have their baggage cleared without inspection or delay. Since they traveled with many bags and trunks and also with a variety of plants and several shepherd dogs, this was a great convenience. But even so, their landing was made impossible by a thick fog. Martha wrote the following description of the end of their crossing:

"After beating about three days, the captain, a bold as well as an experienced seaman, determined to run in at a venture, without having seen the Capes. The ship came near running upon what was conjectured to be the Middle Ground, when anchor was cast at ten o'clock P.M. The wind rose, and the vessel drifted down, dragging her anchor, one or more miles. But she had got within the Capes, while a number which had been less bold were blown off the coast, some of them lost, and all kept out three or four weeks longer. We had to beat up against a strong head-wind, which carried away our topsails; and were very near being run down by a brig coming out of port, which, having the wind in her favor, was almost upon us before we could get out of the way. We escaped, however, with only the loss of a part of our rigging. My father had been so anxious about his public accounts, that he would not trust them to go until he went with them. We arrived at Norfolk in the forenoon, and in two hours after landing, before an article of our baggage was brought ashore, the vessel took fire, and seemed on the point of being reduced to a mere hull. They were in the act of scuttling her, when some abatement in the flames was discovered, and she was finally saved. So great had been the activity of her crew, and those belonging to other ships in the harbor who came to their aid, that everything in her was saved. Our trunks, and perhaps also the papers, had been put in our state-rooms, and the doors incidentally closed by the captain. They were so close that the flames did not penetrate; but the powder in a musket in one of them was silently consumed, and the thickness of the travelling-trunks alone saved their contents from the excessive heat. I understood at the time that the state-room alone, of all the internal partitions escaped burning. . . .

"There were no stages in those days. We were indebted to the kindness of our friends for horses . . . we reached Monticello on the 23d of December. The negroes discovered the approach of the carriage as soon as it reached Shadwell [four miles distant from Monticello], and such a scene I never witnessed in my life. They collected in crowds around it, and almost drew it up the mountain by hand. The shouting, etc., had been sufficiently obstreperous before, but the moment it arrived at the top it reached the climax. When the door of the carriage was opened, they received him in their arms and bore him to the house, crowding around and kissing his hands and feet—some blubbering and crying—others laughing. It seemed impossible to satisfy their anxiety to touch and kiss the very earth which bore him. These were the first ebullitions of joy for his return, after a long absence, which they would of course feel; but perhaps it is not out of place here to add that they were at all times very devoted in their attachment to him."

Corroboration of this last comment of Martha Jefferson's comes from an authoritative source. Isaac Jefferson, one of Jefferson's slaves, has left us his reminiscences of his master. They were dictated to Charles Campbell, the Virginia historian, and taken down by him in 1840. Isaac had lived at Monticello, where he was born in 1775, until 1824, or two years before Thomas Jefferson's death. He describes him as

" '. . . a tall, strait-bodied man as ever you see, right square-shouldered. Nary man in this town walked so straight as my Old Master; neat a built man as ever was seen in Vaginny, I reckon, or any place—a straight up-man, long face, high nose. . . . Old Master wore Vaginny cloth and a red waistcoat, (all the gentlemen wore red waistcoats in dem days) and small clothes, arter dat he used to wear red breeches too.

" 'Old Master was never seen to come out before breakfast—about—8 o'clock. If it was warm weather he wouldn't ride out till evening: studied upstairs till bell ring for dinner. When writing he had a copyin' machine. While he was a-writin' he wouldn't suffer nobody to come into his room. Had a dumb-waiter; when he wanted anything he had nothin to do but turn a crank and the dumb-waiter would bring him water or fruit on a plate or anything he wanted. Old Master had abundance of books; sometimes would have twenty of 'em down on the floor at once—read fust one, then tother. . . . when they go to him to ax him anything, he go right straight to the book and tell you all about it. . . .' "

Other observations of Isaac's about his master give us further views of him:

" 'Mr. Jefferson bowed to everybody he meet. . . . he want rich himself—only his larnin'. . . . never went into the kitchen except to wind up the clock. . . . never heard of his being disguised in drink. . . . Wouldn't shoot a hare settin', nuther; skeer him up fust. . . . never had nothing to do with horse racing or cockfighting. . . . When Old Master heard hunters in the park, he used to go down thar wid his gun and order 'em out. . . . Mr. Jefferson always singing when ridin' or walkin'; hardly see him anywhar outdoors but what he was a-singin'. Had a fine clear voice; sung minuits and sich; fiddled in the parlor. Old Master very kind to servants.' "

There seems little doubt of the truth of old Isaac's observation. Jefferson was indeed a kind master, but his views about the Negro would undoubtedly offend many a present-day liberal or social reformer. He did not believe, as his friend Benjamin Rush did, that the black man is the white man's brother, either by crea-

tion or by redemption. On the contrary, Jefferson always remained ambivalent about the concept of equality. He abhorred
the institution of slavery, and yet he kept slaves and was by no
means the first in Virginia to set them free. His excuse would
have been that the system of agriculture then existing on a Virginia plantation required slave labor, especially in the face of a
rapidly depreciating agricultural market.

This was one of his many rationalizations about the blacks.
One cannot escape the feeling that he was attracted to them, even
sexually; but these feelings were "ego-alien" and had to be pushed
aside. The result was a conflict in his feelings which he was never
able to reconcile and which led to confusion and guilt.

He recognized fully that the problem he faced was an insoluble
one, as indeed we today are being forced to recognize. He put it
boldly by saying: "We have the wolf by the ears, and we can neither hold him nor safely let him go. Justice is in one scale, and
self-preservation in the other."

He was never quite clear, and certainly not explicit, as to
whether Negroes were of the same species as the whites, and, in
any case, he left no doubt that in his view the Negro was not the
equal of the white man, nor could he become so. The thought of
the sexual mixture of Negroes with whites caused him feelings of
deep repugnance. The "improvement" in the fruit of such a union
was evidence to him that the inferiority of the black man was
idiosyncratic, not merely the result of the condition of his life. In
truth, he placed the Negro on nature's scale at a point midway between the white man and the orangutan, thus consigning him to a
role both more aggressive and more animal than the white man's.
Even Jefferson's friend Dr. Rush, with all his scientific pretensions, held the popular view that African women had been de-
bauched by apes and given birth to Negroes. More than this,
Rush suspected that the black color of Negroes derived from lep-
rosy, and this fact entitled them to a double portion of our humanity and compassion. If the color of Negroes is a disease, he
reasoned, then let science and humanity combine in their efforts
to find a cure for it.

Jefferson held out no such utopian dream. On the contrary, he was convinced that an amalgamation of Negroes with whites would result in a degradation in the human character to which no lover of excellence could consent. Although he granted that they are at least as brave and more adventuresome than whites, this fact, he thought, arose from a want of forethought which prevented them from seeing danger until it was upon them. And when it came, they reacted to it with no more coolness or steadiness.

The difference of color and "perhaps of faculty" he found to be a powerful obstacle to their emancipation. When freed, he felt they must be removed "beyond the reach of mixture," and he favored deporting them to Africa and providing them with all encouragement plus the implements of agriculture. He favored filling the vacancies left by the deported Negroes with white settlers.

He spoke of the deep-rooted prejudices entertained by the whites and the ten thousand recollections by the blacks of the injuries they had sustained. The differences between the races "will divide us into parties, and produce convulsions, which will probably never end but in the extermination of the one or the other race."

Jefferson was caught again, as he had been before, in the perilous dilemma between his head and his heart. He wanted above all to be just and generous and kind, but he bolstered his prejudices with arguments which he liked to think were fixed and inherent in the very nature of the blacks. He said of them that their love was more "an eager desire than a tender mixture of sentiment and sensation." Their griefs he thought were transient. Their afflictions were less felt and sooner forgotten. In memory they were equal to the whites, he thought, but in reason much inferior. Scarcely one could be found capable of understanding Euclid. He summed up his views by declaring them dull in imagination and tasteless. Compared to the Indians they were backward indeed, not only in the graphic and plastic arts but in oratory. He had never found a black who could utter a thought above the level of plain narration; and he never saw even an elementary talent for painting or sculpture among Negroes. Neither the misery which they had suffered aplenty, nor their love, could find proper outlets in poetry. All this led Jefferson to the suspicion—as he called it—that the blacks are inferior to the whites in the endowments both of body and mind, and this in turn was a powerful obstacle to their emancipation. One can only read this bill of particulars with amazement, but one should bear in mind that a southern gentleman and landowner today dependent for his livelihood on Negro labor might find himself uttering rather similar sentiments. Even with all his nobility and sense of justice, Thomas Jefferson was, of course, a child of his times and of his culture. And in this culture a liberal education was still the privilege of a very few.

To return to the slave, Isaac, he said of "Miss Martha" (Jefferson's daughter) that she was a "mighty peaceable woman; never holler for servant; make no fuss nor racket; pity she ever died!"

Martha was now a tall and stately-looking girl of seventeen, much resembling her father, and Maria a beautiful girl of eleven. The three of them—father and daughters—were at last safely settled in their beloved Monticello. It was Jefferson's firm and avowed intention to live there in retirement and devote himself to his family, his farms, and his studies. That was the life he loved above all others. But the needs of his country would not allow him to withdraw from public life. He was repeatedly torn between his love of rural life and retirement, on the one hand, and his need to play an active part in the life of his country, on the other. Looked at psychologically, this conflict represents the battle between two sides of Jefferson's nature—the masculine and the feminine.

On the way to Monticello from Norfolk he had stopped in Chesterfield County to pay a visit to Mrs. Eppes, his late wife's sister. There he received a letter from General Washington telling him that Washington had nominated him for secretary of state and urging him to accept the appointment without demur.

Washington had been inaugurated president in New York on April 30, 1789, seven months before Jefferson's return home. Years later in his *Autobiography* Jefferson was to write that all he had wanted then was "to sink into the bosom of my family and friends, and devote myself to studies more congenial to my mind."

But this was not to be; he was not only duty-bound, but Washington, for whom he had an almost worshipful admiration, was a man of gentle tact and reasonableness and of enormous persuasive power. The president's letter said:

"I consider the successful administration of the general Government as an object of almost infinite consequence to the present and future happiness of the citizens of the United States. I consider the office of Secretary for the Department of State as *very* important on many accounts: and I know of no person, who, in my judgment could better execute the duties of it than yourself."

In the face of such a request, what could Jefferson do other than to accede to the president's wishes? Many others agreed with Washington's choice and applauded it. Jefferson was not one who could fly in the face of public opinion, to which he was always acutely sensitive, particularly when expressed by President Washington, whose word was always law to him.

Madison rode over to Monticello from Orange County, not only to greet and welcome back his old friend, but also to urge him to accept the appointment without delay. He spoke of the universal enthusiasm for his acceptance and said it would be more conducive to the general good than anything else he could do.

Jefferson greatly loved and admired James Madison. He admired him for his habit of self-possession, for "the rich resources of his luminous and discriminating mind," for his extensive information, and especially for his "pure and spotless virtue." No doubt Madison's words of encouragement strongly inclined Jefferson to accept the appointment. Finally, on December 15, 1789, he sent his reluctant acceptance to the president, saying:

"But it is not for an individual to choose his post. You are to marshal us as may be best for the public good. . . . my chief comfort will be to work under your eye, my only shelter the authority of your name, and the wisdom of measures to be dictated by you and implicitly executed by me."

He found in Washington the strong father figure that he craved, and so he agreed to take office in March.

Before setting out for New York, Jefferson gave away his eldest daughter, Martha, in marriage. The bridegroom was Thomas

Mann Randolph of Tuckahoe, who had been the ward of Colonel Peter Jefferson, Martha's grandfather. The betrothal was very much a family affair and met the enthusiastic approval of the bride's father. Young Randolph had visited the Jeffersons in Paris after he had finished his studies at the University of Edinburgh, and there the young people had fallen in love. They were married by the Reverend Mr. Maury of the Episcopal Church, son of Thomas Jefferson's own boyhood teacher.

A few days after the wedding, Jefferson set out for New York by way of Richmond. He was delayed in his travels by a snowfall of eighteen inches, and so he sent his carriage to New York by water and found a seat, instead, in the stage, having his horses led. Because of the muddy condition of the roads, it took all of a fortnight to travel from Richmond to New York. The coach could seldom go more than two to three miles an hour, and at night, only one. He arrived in Philadelphia on March 17 and went at once to call on Benjamin Franklin, who was by that time bedridden. Jefferson referred to him in his *Memoir* as "the venerable and beloved Franklin." The old gentleman was curious to learn the fate of the many friends he had left behind him in France, and Jefferson tried to enlighten him, but the conversation was almost too much for Franklin's strength.

Jefferson then proceeded to New York, arriving on March 21. He found temporary lodgings at the City Tavern. His first object was to look for a house on Broadway, which he called the center of his business, but finding none vacant, he took a small one belonging to Robert Peter Bruce at 57 Maiden Lane. Alexander Hamilton, with whom he would soon be closely, if painfully, associated, lived nearby on Pine Street, where there are still so many lawyers' offices; and Aaron Burr practiced the law on Nassau Street, near Wall, where he enjoyed a large garden and a grapery. A mass of business awaited Jefferson's arrival. His salary was $3,500 a year, or $500 more than that of any of his colleagues in the cabinet. With little assistance and a very small budget for new appointments, the secretary found himself all but swamped with work. Within a few weeks after his arrival in New York, Jefferson wrote a letter, dated April 2, 1790, to his old friend Lafayette.

"Behold me, my dear friend," it began, "elected Secretary of State, instead of returning to the far more agreeable position which placed me in the daily participation of your friendship. . . . I have been here these ten days harnessed in my new gear. . . ." Jefferson had had no news from France for three months, and then he heard that the Revolution was going along at a steady pace, meeting occasional difficulties and dangers; "but we are not translated from despotism to liberty on a feather bed." He had no fear for the ultimate result, although he was naturally worried about the fate of his friend.

At the same time, Jefferson wrote to Madame de Corny, telling her that on his arrival home he had found his name in the papers announcing his appointment as secretary of state; and that he found it better to sacrifice his own inclination to the will of others.

In another letter to France he wrote on the same day to the Comtesse d'Houdetót, familiar to us through Rousseau's *Confessions:* "I found our friend Franklin in his bed—cheerful and free from pain, but still in his bed. He took a lively interest in the details I gave him of your revolution. I observed his face often flushed in the course of it. He is much emaciated."

Three weeks later he wrote to a Monsieur Grand:

"The good old Dr. Franklin, so long the ornament of our country, and I may say of the world, has at length closed his eminent career. He died on the 17th instant, of an imposthume of his lungs, which having suppurated and burst, he had not strength to throw off the matter, and was suffocated by it. His illness from this imposthume was of sixteen days.* Congress wear mourning for him, by a resolve of their body."

About a year after Franklin's death, Jefferson sent a message to the president of the National Assembly in France. He wrote:

"I have it in charge from the President of the United States of America, to communicate to the National Assembly of France the

* The word "imposthume" is no longer used in medicine. It means an abscess. A lung abscess is a miserable affliction. In Franklin's case, the abscess seems to have broken through into the bronchi and thus made it impossible for him to breathe.

peculiar sensibility of Congress to the tribute paid to the memory of Benjamin Franklin by the enlightened and free representatives of a great nation, in their decree of the 11th of June, 1790.

"That the loss of such a citizen should be lamented by us among whom he lived, whom he so long and eminently served, and who feel their country advanced and honored by his birth, life, and labors, was to be expected. But it remained for the National Assembly of France to set the first example of the representatives of one nation doing homage, by a public act, to the private citizen of another, and, by withdrawing arbitrary lines of separation, to reduce into one fraternity the good and the great, wherever they have lived and died."

CHAPTER THIRTEEN

❧ ❦

Jefferson now found himself in a political atmosphere in New York which he had not in the least expected. He had left France in the first year of her revolution with a great zeal for reformation. At home, he had been cordially received by the president and welcomed by his colleagues and by a circle of the principal citizens. He was the guest of honor at numerous dinner parties, but he admitted that the conversation around the table was often mortifying and filled him with consternation. Politics was the chief topic of conversation, and a great preference for monarchy over a republican form of government was evidently the favorite sentiment. He was almost alone as an outspoken advocate of republicanism, being, of course, neither an apostate nor a hypocrite. New York was the loyalist stronghold in America, and in some counties a Whig was rarely met with. The wealthy and aristocratic families who were now wining and dining Thomas Jefferson had been as hospitable and attentive to the British officers during the occupation. These same families had taken on, perhaps from close association, much of the coloring and manners of the dashing colonels and baronets whom they had received into their houses and with whom their wives and daughters had danced and flirted. In any case, Jefferson smelled out loyalists and monarchists on all sides, to his great distress.

Even some of his colleagues in the president's cabinet had professed strong monarchist views, but Washington was determined to select a cabinet that would be politically balanced. In Jefferson's mind, however, lurked a mistrust that there was a party in the United States bound on overthrowing republicanism. This was his firm conviction, although his adversaries were equally persuaded that he distorted the facts and colored them to his own liking, especially in his suspicions of Hamilton, the secretary of the treasury, whom he considered the head of the opposing group. It must be kept in mind that Jefferson's political ambitions, though still latent, were not negligible.

In Alexander Hamilton he found a man of his own mettle, but one with an overweening pride and ambition and self-esteem, who, even at the age of twelve, had declared that he "would willingly risk his life, though not his character, to exalt his station." In view of subsequent events, this remark was prophetic. John Adams referred to him quite inaccurately as "the bastard brat of a Scotch pedlar." With little more than the rudiments of an education, he soon found himself on a footing of intimacy with the great and influential, through his own brilliance and energy and personal charm. His writings for the press attracted attention and won him the support of the governor and some of the leading citizens of Nevis, the island in the West Indies where he was born. They sent him to New York to continue his education as a special student at King's College (Columbia College). Although a loyalist to begin with, as early as his seventeenth year he became a strong supporter of republicanism and an able pamphleteer. In March 1777, at the age of twenty-two, he was appointed aide-de-camp by General Washington, with the rank of lieutenant colonel. He continued in this post for four years, when he withdrew because of his dislike of the kind of personal dependence that this office entailed. But he was loyal to "the General," as he called him, whom he considered a very honest man, far more so than his competitors, who, he thought, had "slender abilities, and less integrity." Hamilton judged that Washington's popularity was essential to the safety of America, and for this reason he was willing to support him. In 1781, however, a breach in their relationship developed. In spite of Washington's overtures, Hamilton declined to remain in his service. We next find him with the rank of colonel of the line, commanding a detachment at Yorktown with conspicuous bravery. The year before he had married Elizabeth, daughter of General Philip Schuyler of New York. The Schuylers were rich, influential, and aristocratic patroons. By espousing one of them, Hamilton, in characteristic fashion, both elevated and secured his own social position and feathered his nest. Probably because of the Schuyler influence, his political sentiments now underwent a second metamorphosis; he emerged an embattled Anglophile and royalist, with little patience or respect for the common people and nothing but contempt for the democratic ideal. Mankind in general he thought was vicious, and the people were to him "a great beast."

He was admitted to the bar after only a few months' study and was elected to Congress in 1782. Four years later he was one of the two delegates chosen from New York to attend the Constitutional Convention in Annapolis.

This was the man with whom Jefferson's fortunes were soon to be closely interwoven. Although antipodal in their habits of thought and their social philosophies, Jefferson never underestimated Hamilton's great gifts and referred to him as a "colossus." It was inevitable, however, that the two should clash. Between them there were differences in breeding, taste, and ideals that remained irreconcilable. Whereas Jefferson was quiet and steady, Hamilton was excitable and volatile. Whereas Jefferson was a born aristocrat and gentleman, Hamilton was a careerist and a social climber. Whereas Jefferson was an American through and through, rooted in the fruitful and fertile acres of his native Virginia, Hamilton always remained an alien, more at home in the financial world of the big northern cities than in the plantations of the South.

Even their physical configurations were contrasted: Hamilton, an aggressive bantam; Jefferson, tall, slender, and rather stiff in his manner. With all his tolerance and charity, Jefferson could never understand his younger associate—far less like him. We should therefore not judge him through Jefferson's eyes. He considered Hamilton an upstart and a snob, "not only a monarchist, but for a monarchy bottomed on corruption," interested in money and power, not in liberty and equality. Jefferson's heroes were Bacon, Newton, and Locke, who were, in his opinion, "the three greatest men the world had ever produced"; but for Hamilton, the greatest man that ever lived was Julius Caesar.

Both men were firmly attached to Washington. Hamilton, in spite of his ambitious restiveness, knew which side his bread was buttered on; Jefferson was tied to the president by deep respect and ancient loyalty. Since the president was no expert in fiscal matters, he allowed much scope to Hamilton, who soon developed a large and thriving department with seventy subordinates by the end of 1790, while Jefferson had only five. And yet Washington recognized that the state department embraced nearly all the objects of administration, and so he greatly relied on his fellow Virginian.

Later in life, after Washington's death, Jefferson wrote an analysis of his character which reveals much about both men:

"I think I knew George Washington intimately and thoroughly. . . .

"His mind was great and powerful, without being of the very first order; his penetration strong, though not so acute as that of a Newton, Bacon, or Locke; and as far as he saw, no judgment was ever sounder. It was slow in operation, being little aided by invention or imagination, but sure in conclusion . . . hearing all suggestions, he selected whatever was best; and certainly no General ever planned his battles more judiciously. . . . He was incapable of fear, meeting personal dangers with calmest unconcern.

"Perhaps the strongest feature in his character was prudence, never acting until every circumstance, every consideration, was maturely weighed. . . . His integrity was most pure, his justice the most inflexible I have ever known, no motives of interest or consanguinity, of friendship or hatred, being able to bias his decision. He was, indeed, in every sense of the words, a wise, a good, and a great man. His temper was naturally high toned; but reflection and resolution had obtained a firm and habitual ascendency of it. If ever, however, it broke its bonds, he was most tremendous in wrath.

"In his expenses he was honorable, but exact; liberal in contributions to whatever promised utility; but frowning and unyielding on all visionary projects and all unworthy calls on his charity. His heart was not warm in its affections; but he exactly calculated every man's value, and gave him a solid esteem proportioned to it.

"His person, you know, was fine, his stature exactly what one would wish, his deportment easy, erect and noble; the best horseman of his age, and the most graceful figure that could be seen on horseback.

"Although in the circle of his friends, where he might be unreserved with safety, he took a free share in conversation, his colloquial talents were not above mediocrity, possessing neither copiousness of ideas, nor fluency of words. In public, when called on for a sudden opinion, he was unready, short and embarrassed. Yet he wrote readily, rather diffusely, in an easy and correct style. This he had acquired by conversation with the world, for his education was merely reading, writing, and common arithmetic, to which he added surveying at a later day. His time was employed in action chiefly, reading little, and that only in agriculture and English history. . . . His correspondence . . . with his agricultural proceedings, occupied most of his leisure hours within doors.

"On the whole, his character was, in its mass, perfect, in nothing bad, in few points indifferent; and it may truly be said, that never did nature and fortune combine more perfectly to make a man great, and to place him in . . . an everlasting remembrance."

Jefferson's dispassionate perceptiveness combined with his capacity for empathy and his felicitous use of the language makes his portrayal of Washington come alive. The statuesque president held a median position between the two protagonists—the secretary of state and the secretary of the treasury—so that for a while, at least, they were able to collaborate.

It was Jefferson's custom to hold conferences at dinner. After the table had been cleared and the wine or Madeira had been laid on, the genial host would encourage his well-fed guests to discuss their differences. It was the method he had used so effectively during his ministerial duties in France.

A matter of urgent importance now presented itself: Where to locate the national capital? Feelings were strong between the North and South, and there were even threats of secession. A compromise was reached to which Jefferson and Hamilton both agreed, and it was decided to settle on Philadelphia for a ten-year period.

This compromise was the result of the now-familiar process of logrolling. The North had agreed to the establishment of the federal capital on the Potomac, and in return for this Hamilton's Assumption Bill was adopted. It provided for the federal government's assuming the war debts of the various states. Jefferson recognized the danger of bankruptcy and of loss of credit in Europe, and so he reluctantly supported Hamilton's measure. Again, Jefferson acted as mediator. He invited the secretary of the treasury to dine with him, together with Richard Bland Lee and Alexander White, both Congressmen from Virginia. The southern gentlemen, in return for placing the capital near their state, agreed to switch their votes and to support the Assumption Bill.

This was a rough stretch for Jefferson, unaccustomed as he was to political horse-trading. Moreover, he disliked New York; he was overworked and lonesome and craved the affection and warmth of his devoted daughters and his fireside. They would have been balm to his spirits, which were jaded and galled by the raw persistence of the secretary of the treasury, whom he fought —at least as he felt—not out of personal grudge but out of firm convictions. His health now began to suffer. One could almost venture a diagnosis from the meticulous, duty-bound character of the man and the conflict in which he was trapped. Here were all the conditions for migraine headaches, and in truth he was incapacitated for business during the whole month of May, although he remained at his post. For two or three days at a time he was prostrated from the effects of severe headaches.

To add to Jefferson's worries came word that the president himself was alarmingly sick. For several days in May his recovery was despaired of. The inner circle of official persons close to him had almost given up hope when he rallied and began slowly to improve. On May 23, 1790, a letter to Maria, not quite twelve years old, from her father said: "Tell your uncle that the President, after having been so ill as at one time to be thought dying, is now quite recovered. I have been these three weeks confined by periodical headache. It has been the most moderate I ever had, but it has not yet left me."

On May 26, 1790, Jefferson wrote his former secretary, Short, saying that he had been tortured for a month by one of his periodic headaches.

Jefferson himself was described by Senator Maclay of Pennsylvania in words which reveal a mixture of tension and relaxation, as though he were trying to shake off one of these attacks. Jefferson was "a slender man; has rather the air of stiffness in his manner; his clothes seem too small for him; he sits in a lounging manner, on one hip commonly, and with one of his shoulders elevated much above the other; his face has a sunny aspect; his whole figure has a loose shackling air. . . . He had a rambling, vacant look, and nothing of that firm collected deportment which I expected would dignify the presence of a secretary or minister. I looked for gravity but a laxity of manner seemed shed about him. He spoke almost without ceasing. But even his discourse partook of his personal demeanor. It was loose and rambling, yet he scattered information wherever he went, and some even brilliant sentiments sparked from him. The information he gave us respecting foreign ministers etc. was all high-spiced." And then the senator added: "He has been long enough abroad to catch the tone of European folly."

Communications with his daughters at this time reveal, as usual, his constant concern and his worrisome devotion.

To Martha Jefferson Randolph, written in New York on April 4, 1790:

"I am anxious to hear from you of your health, your occupations, where you are, etc. Do not neglect your music. It will be a companion which will sweeten many hours of life to you. I assure you mine here is triste enough. Having had yourself and dear

Poll to live with me so long, to exercise my affections and cheer me in the intervals of business, I feel heavily the separation from you. It is a circumstance of consolation to know that you are happier, and to see a prospect of its continuance in the prudence and even temper of Mr. Randolph and yourself. Your new condition will call for abundance of little sacrifices. But they will be greatly overpaid by the measure of affection they secure to you. The happiness of your life now depends on the continuing to please a single person. To this all other objects must be secondary, even your love for me, were it possible that could ever be an obstacle. But this it never can be. Neither of you can ever have a more faithful friend than myself, nor one on whom you can count for more sacrifices. My own is become a secondary object to the happiness of you both. Cherish, then, for me, my dear child, the affection of your husband, and continue to love me as you have done, and to render my life a blessing by the prospect it may hold up to me of seeing you happy. Kiss Maria for me if she is with you, and present me cordially to Mr. Randolph [her husband!]; assuring yourself of the constant and unchangeable love of yours, affectionately.

Th. Jefferson."

A week later he wrote to Maria, directing her to "answer me all these questions": Did she see the sun rise every day? How many pages of *Don Quixote* did she read each day, and how far advanced in him was she? Did she repeat a grammar lesson every day? What else did she read? How many hours a day did she sew? Had she had an opportunity to continue her music? Did she know how to make a pudding yet? To cut out a beefsteak, to sow spinach, or to set a hen? And then he continued with his familiar hortative advice:

"Be good, my dear, as I have always found you; never be angry with any body, nor speak harm of them, try to let every body's faults be forgotten, as you would wish yours to be; take more pleasure in giving what is best to another than in having it yourself, and then all the world will love you, and I more than all the world."

A month later he wrote Maria again, saying that her last letter had told him what she was *not* doing, not reading *Don Quixote,* not applying to her music; and he said he was hoping that in her next she would tell him what she *was* doing.

Maria replied:

"I have not been able to read Don Quixote every day, as I have been travelling ever since I saw you last, and the dictionary is too large to go in the packet of the chariot, nor have I yet had an opportunity of continuing my music. I am now reading Robertson's America. I thank you for the advice you were so good as to give me, and will try to follow it. Adieu, my dear papa, I am your affectionate daughter,

Maria Jefferson"

And he to her on July 4, 1790:

"I have written you, my dear Maria, four letters since I have been here, and I have received from you only two.* You owe me two, then, and the present will make three. This is a kind of debt I will not give up. You may ask how I will help myself. By petitioning your aunt, as soon as you receive a letter, to make you go without your dinner till you have answered it."

One doubts that he would ever deprive her so.

Soon he would find relief from his anxiety. In September, five months after becoming secretary of state, Mr. Jefferson returned to Monticello to recuperate in the health-giving warmth of his home.

* The parental plaint has not changed much in a century and four fifths.

CHAPTER FOURTEEN

❧ ❦

After two months' stay at his beloved Monticello, Jefferson, his health fortunately restored, returned to his duties. He left his home on October 12, 1790, stopping at Mount Vernon on the way to Philadelphia, to which in the meanwhile the capital had been moved. His daughter Maria traveled with him and remained with him as long as he was secretary of state. In November 1790 Jefferson, a frugal widower, settled down in a rented house with Maria. Their establishment in Philadelphia consisted of a steward, a maid for Maria, four or five male servants, and a stable of five horses. The change must have been a relief to him, because from the start he had faced New York and its high-flown Tory society with reluctance and dread. Soon he was immersed in his work and in a sea of official papers.

At cabinet meetings he sat to the right of the president, who remained august and inaccessible, reserved and aristocratic, dressed in his beautifully tailored English broadcloth; Jefferson himself in his red Parisian waistcoat, with smallclothes to match, sat opposite Alexander Hamilton, then only thirty-three years old, who was at the president's left. Washington was fifty-eight years old, and though in some ways perhaps not richly endowed, he was infinitely patient and just and willing to listen to all sides of a subject, feeling deeply his need of help from his associates. Jefferson, who was forty-seven, quiet, unobtrusive, and the least pugnacious man, found that he and Hamilton were "pitted against each other like two fighting cocks." Jefferson called him "the evil genius of America"; and George Mason, who took an active part in drafting the Constitution, said that Hamilton had done the country more harm than "Great Britain with all her fleets and armies."

If he had his bitter critics, Hamilton had as many friends and admirers. In speaking of him, Daniel Webster agreed that he alone caused the moribund public credit to come to life, and General Meade addressed him with affectionate devotion, while Washington prized him for his fluent tongue, his ready pen, and his quick mind for figures, the very talents that were wanting in the president.

Hamilton, positive, vehement, and inflexible, standing but five feet seven inches tall, has been described as a public figure, by nature commanding, self-sufficient, and condescending, even to Washington, who moved and talked to the strings that Hamilton pulled behind the green curtain. Arrogant and irreconcilably averse to the town-meeting spirit, he dearly loved the military and slept by preference in a tent on his own lawn. Without respect for the common soldier, he believed passionately in an aristocratic officer class and discoursed interminably on the charms of monarchy. He is quoted as saying, "Every day proves to me, more and more, that this American world was not made for me." No less beguiled by the trappings of monarchy with its splendor and majesty was John Adams, who became vice president in 1789. He thought the French Revolution wholly diabolical. General Knox, the secretary of war, a bookseller in Boston by trade, became the perfect model of the military man. He favored abolishing the state governments and establishing in their place a strong, imposing general government, with plenty of soldiers to enforce its decrees. In all matters of public policy he was the mere echo of Hamilton, whose faith in the apparatus of finance was equaled only by Knox's faith in guns. Edmund Randolph of Virginia, who had been disinherited by his father for siding with the Revolution, was the attorney-general. Jefferson said of him that he sometimes gave the shells to his friends and the oysters to the enemy.

This was the group about Washington. Because of his unassailable dignity, and although anti-monarchist, he still was surrounded by an aura of kingship, in spite of having invented for himself the appellation "Mr. President." The story is told about him that at an evening entertainment Alexander Hamilton had wagered with Gouverneur Morris that he would not dare slap the president on the back. The stakes were to be a supper and wine for a dozen of Morris's friends. On the appointed evening Morris entered the room where the president was receiving, bowed, shook hands, and laid his left hand on the president's shoulder, saying, "My dear General, I am very happy to see you look so well!" At this, Washington withdrew his hand, stepped back, fixed his eye on Morris for several minutes with an angry frown, whereupon Morris shrank away and tried to lose himself in the crowd. At the dinner which Hamilton provided, Morris is quoted as saying, "I have won the bet, but paid dearly for it, and nothing could induce me to repeat it."

General Washington rode out in a cream-colored coach drawn by six horses and attended by white servants (some historians say they were black) liveried in white cloth trimmed with scarlet. What a contrast to Jefferson, who rode to his own inauguration unattended, dismounted, and hung the bridle of his horse on a paling outside the Capitol!

Two men as different as Hamilton and Jefferson, the one a man of action, the other a man of intellect, were bound to disagree and perhaps eventually to come into open conflict. Before long they found themselves on opposite sides of most of the issues that pressed upon the young country. Jefferson has been accorded a hero's wreath as the true author of American democracy, while Hamilton never quite won his place among the Founding Fathers. He was too young, he came too late, and he was an alien of allegedly mixed parentage. It is possible that Jefferson, in spite of his accustomed magnanimity, was jealous of this brilliant rival, this younger sibling competing for the love and indulgence of the great, all-wise father. He did, to be sure, appreciate Hamilton's genius, referring to him in a letter to Madison as "an host, within himself."

No one can deny Hamilton's great accomplishments, but great accomplishments seldom make a man lovable. A recent biographer, Clinton Rossiter, lists some of them. First, he was the financier, who acknowledged the Revolutionary debt and engineered the assumption of the state debts and their funding. He imposed and collected the first federal taxes, introduced a viable currency and the establishment of bimetallism. He created and administered the Treasury Department and launched the Bank of the United States, thereby securing the public credit of a "virtually friendless government." He has been called "the greatest administrative genius of his generation in America and one of the greatest administrators of all time." Impatient, arrogant, meddlesome, and intolerant of competition, he was nevertheless conspicuous for his energy and industry, for his originality, and for his phenomenal capacity to inspire confidence. If Jefferson was one side of the medal, Hamilton was its reverse. It is no wonder that the two men could not see eye to eye. Hamilton had little of the soft, tender, artistic, aesthetic, and feminine in his makeup that characterized his rival. In the face of this kind of indwelling opposition, it is fair enough to look for deeper causes for their hostility and to suspect an intense if threatening attraction between them. But this is speculation, though familiar enough to students of personality.

Hamilton was first and foremost a realist and the apostle of enlightened self-interest, "the prophet of industrial America, a man who dwelled in the midst of a race of agrarians and dared to tell them that their future was bound up in ships, counting houses, banks, highways, canals, and, above all, factories." This is the America we live in, and whether we like it or not, Hamilton was and is still its presiding genius—evil to Jefferson and to those who, like him, cherished or cherish another dream. In a sense, Americans have been trying to choose between them every four years ever since. But they need both. As Walter Lippmann has put it with telling perspicacity, "to be partisan today as between Jefferson and Hamilton is like arguing whether men or women are more necessary to the procreation of the race." Both were vital to the development of the country: Hamilton, with his astute mind; Jefferson, with his creative genius.

If Hamilton was a financial genius, Jefferson was far from it. He seems always to have been rather bored by the notion of budgeting, in spite of the careful accounting of his private expenditures. At this time in his life (the first quarter of 1791) he had a personal deficit of more than a hundred dollars a month on a monthly salary of three hundred. His expenses have been itemized thus: thirty-eight dollars for rent; thirty-two dollars for his stable; forty-four dollars for food; services, including laundry, twenty-nine dollars; and firewood, twenty-four dollars. The cost of living was high. Coffee, for example, cost $3.20 per pound. In his meticulous, if not fussy, way, Jefferson figured that every time he served a cup of coffee with sugar it cost him two cents, and so, since tea cost only two dollars a pound, he served tea instead, which amounted to 1.6 cents per cup, or a saving of 0.4 cents. He had recorded in his account-book that on March 8 he was out of tea and that the pound had lasted him exactly seven weeks, used six times per week. What he served on the seventh day of rest he does not confide to us.

In addressing himself to his new duties as secretary of state, he concentrated, among other things, on establishing a diplomatic service. He wrote to all existing consuls charging them to send him every six months a list of all vessels entering their ports and a description of their cargoes. He also requested information of any military preparations or other indications of war. He cautioned them to husband the good dispositions of the governments to which they were assigned and to make all representations to them in "the most temperate and friendly terms, never indulging in any case whatever in a single expression that may irritate."

He was deeply concerned lest under Hamilton's leadership financial speculators, or "stock-jobbers," as Jefferson called them, would get control of the federal government. Partly as a result of Hamilton's financial policies, a period of prosperity set in. Business was flourishing, but this did not allay Jefferson's worries as he watched farmers being corrupted by merchants and speculators. Concern for liberty and equality gave way, especially in Massachusetts and New York, to concern for money and profits. The secretary of the treasury was on the ascendant—closely associated with what would later be called "big business" and with those members of Congress who supported it. Senator Maclay said of Hamilton that he was "all-powerful, and fail[ed] in nothing he attempt[ed]." Success made Hamilton even more arrogant than he had been before. He stuck his nose into everything and spoke out at cabinet meetings without reserve or consideration for opinions other than his own. In his special field, of finance, he far outshone Jefferson, who made no pretense at being an expert.

President Washington tried as usual to steer a middle course between his two secretaries, but in this instance he could not help supporting the fiscal policies of his secretary of the treasury, especially as Jefferson had no better ones to propose. The cost of the Revolution had been $17.5 million per annum, and the United States debt, as of January 1790, amounted to more than $54 million, which Hamilton looked upon as the price of liberty. The impending financial crisis led to a delirium of speculation, and this situation alarmed even Hamilton. Jefferson's inherent dislike of financial matters was such that he took no part in the strife.

But now the two contending champions began to try to curry public support. The country would soon be divided between their followers—a southern agrarian group under the leadership of Jefferson and a northern commercial group headed by Hamilton. The lines of political battle were drawn, and each side rolled up its field pieces, in the shape of the public press. The captains of the contending artillery were John Fenno of Philadelphia, editor of the *Gazette of the United States,* which became Hamilton's mouthpiece, and Philip Morin Freneau, a classmate of Madison's at Princeton, who had been employed as a translating clerk in the department of state. In October 1791 he came to Philadelphia, where he began to publish the *National Gazette.*

Throughout the heated controversy, which raged between Fenno and Freneau and their two gazettes, Jefferson remained aloof, never so much as providing Freneau with copy or publishing anything under a false name. In fact, he told Adams, then vice president, "I never did in my life, either by myself or by any other, have a sentence of mine inserted in a newspaper without putting my name to it: & I believe I never shall." And to his son-in-law Randolph, he said, "I am determined to let them write and wrangle as they please without intermeddling in word or deed." But he did intermeddle behind the scenes. While his colleagues did the acting, he did the planning, and he saw to it that his plans were carried out. This clandestine behavior made him suspect and gave him the reputation of being sly and untrustworthy. Throughout this excruciatingly trying period, Jefferson never stooped to personal abuse or slander or mean innuendo, although he often must have been tempted.

To support Jefferson's contention, "Freneau published an affidavit declaring that Jefferson had nothing to do with the establishment of his paper, or with his coming to Philadelphia," and that "he had never directly or indirectly written, dictated, or composed a single line for it." But Fenno was not to be silenced; he called Freneau the " 'pensioned tool' " of a " 'public character' " and tried to discredit him, declaring that " 'the facts speak louder than words and under certain circumstances louder than oaths.' "

Jefferson was contemptuously charged with falsehoods, with treachery to the administration, with a desire to repudiate the public debt, and with dishonest business dealings. Hamilton was generally understood to be the author of these attacks. Under the pseudonyms "An American" and "Catullus," he let fly his poisoned barbs at the secretary of state and also at the government. This angered the president, who suggested to Jefferson that he should withdraw Freneau's appointment as translating clerk in his office. "But," Jefferson wrote in his *Anas*, "I will not do it. His paper has saved our Constitution, which was galloping fast into monarchy, and has been checked by no means so powerfully as by that paper. It is well and universally known, that it has been that paper which has checked the career of the monocrats; and the President, not sensible of the designs of the party, has not with his usual good sense and *sang froid*, looked on the efforts and effects of this free press, and seen that, though some bad things have passed through it to the public, yet the good have preponderated immensely."

The *Anas*, so-called, were contained in three volumes bound in marble paper, consisting, among other things, of official opinions given in writing to George Washington by his secretary of state. Very often they were memoranda on loose scraps of paper, ragged, rubbed, and scribbled, and carried in Jefferson's pocket until given to a binder who came to his office to collect them, without the opportunity of reading any of them.

They "will show," wrote the author, "that the contests of that day were contests of principle, between the advocates of republican, and those of kingly government, and that had not the former made the efforts they did, our government would have been, even at this early day, a very different thing from what the successful issue of those efforts have made it."

These notes were begun in his second year as secretary of state, that is, in 1791. It was in this politically heated period that the Federalist party was for a while in the ascendancy under the leadership of Hamilton and Marshall, and that the Republican party was born, with Jefferson at its head, ably assisted by Madison.

Jefferson tried to establish the fact that the Republicans were more than troublemakers and grumblers, but firm advocates of republican rather than kingly government. Sympathy with monarchical principles was rife among the Federalists, while their opponents, the Republicans, saw them as the creatures of privilege and corruption bent on introducing Hamiltonian measures which would gradually but surely ensnare the government in a web "indistinguishable from the English model." Jefferson condemned the Federalists less because they were privileged capitalists than because they were corrupt monarchists. In any case, his personal notes as printed in his *Anas* subjected him to bitter attack and abuse for the century to come. In fact, there have been few political figures in the history of our country about whom passions were so divided.

Sensitive and human as he was, this kind of personal attack on his motives and his honor was quite insupportable to him. His deep distaste for political wrangling and his urgent wish to retire to his Virginia estate finally, on May 23, 1792, caused him to write a letter of nearly three thousand words to the president.

He began by saying that the subject of the letter had for some

time past occasioned him inquietude of mind—the more so because Washington himself had been threatening to retire from the
government.

"I can scarcely contemplate a more incalculable evil than the
breaking of the Union into two or more parts. . . . The confidence of the whole Union is centered in you. Your being at the
helm will be more than an answer to every argument which can
be used to alarm and lead the people in any quarter, into violence and secession. North and South will hang together if they
have you to hang on. . . . I am perfectly aware of the oppression
under which your present office lays your mind, and of the ardor
with which you pant for domestic life."

And then having tried to persuade the president to stay at his
post in spite of exhaustion, he went on to say that his "own inclination, . . . [was] bent irresistibly on the tranquil enjoyment of
my family, my farm, and my books."

The president, quite aware of the smouldering feud between
his two principal cabinet officers, delayed answering this letter
from day to day because the subject of his remaining in office was
so painful to him. After three months, however, he wrote Jefferson on August 23:

"How unfortunate, and how much regretted is it, then, that
while we are encompassed on all sides with avowed enemies, and
insidious friends, internal dissentions should be harrowing and
tearing our vitals."

And then the letter went on in pious and ponderous prose urging the two rivals to bury the hatchet and to make up.

Within three weeks of receiving this letter Jefferson had dispatched his reply to President Washington, from Monticello. Before it reached him, the president had written to Hamilton,
expressing the hope that liberal allowance would be made for differences in political opinion. He did not mince words in this letter, but made it very clear that he was referring to the wounding
and irritating charges that had found their way into the pages of
"some of our Gazettes."

Jefferson, in his reply to Washington, was equally outspoken
and named names. He had been accused in Fenno's *Gazette* of

having opposed the Constitution, of favoring the non-payment of debts, and of "setting up a paper to decry and slander the Government." To all of these charges Jefferson gave the lie. He told the president that when he had come into office it was with a resolution to retire from it as soon as he decently could, and that he looked toward such a time "with a longing of a wave-worn mariner, who has at length the land in view," and counts the days and hours which still lie ahead. He wrote that he would not suffer his retirement "to be clouded by the slanders of a man whose history, from the moment in which history . . . can stoop to notice him, is a tissue of machinations against the liberty of the country which has not only received and given him bread, but heaped its honors on his head." He went on to affirm that not a syllable of the dissensions reported in the newspapers had proceeded from him.

Hamilton's reply to the president's letter was simpler and more straightforward. He accused Jefferson of uniformly opposing him and of circulating " 'unkind whispers and insinuations' " against him. "Nevertheless," he continued, "I pledge my honor to you, sir, that if you shall hereafter form a plan to reunite the members of your administration upon some steady principle of cooperation, I will faithfully concur in executing it during my continuance in office. And I will not directly or indirectly say or do a thing that shall endanger a feud."

One is tempted to take sides in this acrimonious dispute, but to do so would be foolish. Far better for the historian or biographer to look behind the passions which separated these two men, to their underlying characters, where the contrasts were such as to lead to inevitable conflict. The difference in policy between them was less a cause for their mutual hostility than it was the result of it. Hamilton seems to have been the less outraged of the two and in words, at least, the more willing to seek a common meeting ground, even though Jefferson's career in politics had been built on his reputation for fairness and on his constant readiness to compromise. Indeed, he was flexible enough, unless challenged as he was by Hamilton. He would not compromise his republican principles, however, nor yield an inch to systems which to him were both false and dangerous. His ultimate faith was in the enlightened judgment of the people, and for this Hamilton had little more than contempt.

Anyone trained in depth psychology or in psychodynamics will not fail to see in the mutual hostility between Jefferson and Hamilton certain motifs that enter into the lives of many men—although often unbeknownst to them. First, one can detect an overweening competitiveness, in this instance, as we have noted, for the love and approval of an authoritative father figure. The stage was set for just such a battle in Jefferson, who had lost his father at an early age. We know what a lasting influence this stalwart pioneer had had on his son. Hamilton, allegedly the illegitimate son of a sea captain, or, as some say, of a Scottish immigrant, can have had little emotional support from his absent father during his formative years. Both men were left with unsatisfied dependent needs, and both turned to Washington, not without ambivalence, as a living father symbol to satisfy their longings. This brought them into immediate and inevitable conflict. Their rivalry was complicated by their mutual admiration, in which unconscious elements of attraction no doubt entered. This in turn had to be defended against, and it fanned the flames of their mutual enmity. It also led, in Jefferson, to a great reluctance to be competitive and even to assume responsibility, as, for example, in his fiscal policy; and it explains in part his constant wish to withdraw from the battle of political life and to retire to his estates. If he was inept in the management of the public economy, he was meticulously careful in his personal finances, accounting in what looks like a picayune way for the last penny.

Within six days of Hamilton's ever-so-reasonable, conciliatory letter to the chief magistrate, he resumed his vehement personal assault on Jefferson and continued it for many months. Jefferson offered no retaliation; he seldom, if ever, rose to his own defense when attacked.

Jefferson spent the night of September 30 at Mount Vernon and after breakfast had some talk with the president, who was greatly concerned about the friction that had developed between his two chief cabinet officers. He apparently had had no notion that it had become so intense. He expressed great regret at Jefferson's threatened retirement and urged him, then and frequently thereafter, to remain in office in order to "keep things in their proper channel, and prevent them from going too far."

Jefferson told the president that there were many people who had "monarchy in contemplation" and that Alexander Hamilton was one of them. In fact, Jefferson heard Hamilton declare that "this Constitution was a shilly shally thing, of mere milk and water, which could not last, and was only good as a step to something better." But Washington maintained his Olympian detachment. In a letter marked "private" addressed to Jefferson, he wrote: "I have a great, a sincere esteem and regard for you both, and ardently wish that some line may be marked out by which both of you could walk."

But, of course, there was too much discord between them, which culminated in a bitter personal feud. They differed philosophically on the nature and needs of society and government, on the perfectibility of man, on trust in the people to govern themselves through representative institutions. Hamilton upheld the authoritarian view, believing that the people were unfit to govern themselves and were best governed by an elite. There seemed no way of reconciling these differences. Each accused the other of political intrigue and bad faith.

As they disagreed on internal policies, they soon split on foreign affairs as well. Jefferson's sympathies naturally leaned toward France, where he had spent so many gratifying years and where the Revolution had involved him and stirred him. Just as surely did Hamilton lean toward Britain, which represented not only his own origins but also the monarchy he so greatly revered. More than this, France had always been female among the nations, as Britain had been male. Each of these greatly gifted men turned inevitably toward his own image: Jefferson, in whose personality the female was so much in evidence, toward France; and Hamilton, aggressive, imperious, tenacious, and utterly masculine, toward Britain. But the president held firmly to a policy of genuine neutrality, as he was attempting to do between England and France.

Jefferson's term of office was now rapidly approaching its end. He had planned to withdraw at the close of it. The Republicans in Congress urged him to reconsider, but he was weary from the continuous assaults on his character. His estates had suffered greatly from his long absences. His house was still unfinished, and repairs and changes were much needed. For nearly ten years he had been no more than a transient visitor in his own home. If Hamilton had stopped his slanderous abuse at this time, it is possible that his adversary would have left his office for greener pastures, but Jefferson was not one to quit under fire. Except when challenged, as now by Hamilton, he was flexible enough. Each time he considered resigning he would be called back by his sense of duty and also by his need to be loved.

A letter from Philadelphia, dated January 26, 1793, exposes some of his deeper feelings:

"My dear Martha:

I received two days ago yours of the 16th. You were never more mistaken than in supposing you were too long on the prattle, etc. of little Anne. I read it with quite as much pleasure as you write it. I sincerely wish I could hear of her perfect re-establishment. I have for some time past been under an agitation of mind which I scarcely ever experienced before, produced by a check on my purpose of returning home at the close of this session of Congress. My operations at Monticello had been all made to bear upon that point of time; my mind fixed on it with a fondness which was extreme, the purpose firmly declared to the President, when I became assailed from all quarters with a variety of objections. Among these it was urged that my retiring just when I had been attacked in the public papers would injure me in the eyes of the public, who would suppose I either withdrew from investigation, or because I had not tone of mind sufficient to meet slander. The only reward I ever wished on my retirement was, to carry with me nothing like a disapprobation of the public. These representations have for some weeks past shaken a determination which I have thought the whole world could not have shaken. I have not yet finally made up my mind on the subject, nor changed my declaration to the President. But having perfect reliance in the disinterested friendship of some of those who have counselled and urge it strongly; believing they can see and judge better a question between the public and myself than I can, I feel a possibility that I may be detained here into the summer. A few days will decide. In the meantime I have permitted my house to be rented after the middle of March, have sold such of my furniture as would not suit Monticello, and am packing up the rest and storing it ready to be shipped off to Richmond as soon as the season of good sea-weather comes on."

In spite of his wish to retire, the secretary of state had still many weighty matters to deal with. He had received communications from Monsieur de Ternant, the French minister to the United States, that Gouverneur Morris had become *persona non grata* to the French government; Morris was known to be pro-British and hostile to France, those two countries now being in a state of belligerency. He was, moreover, openly royalist in his sympathies and even planned to take part in an attempt to rescue Louis XVI. Jefferson was told that Morris, while in the presence of his servants, had cursed the French ministers as a "set of damned rascals," and predicted that the king would be "replaced on his throne." His unpopularity with the revolutionists made it impossible for Morris to remain as minister.

President Washington therefore recalled him in 1794, after two years of service. To smooth the ruffled French feelings, the president thought of no better expedient than asking Jefferson to return to France at this critical moment, and to remain there for a year or two. Jefferson of all men possessed the confidence of both sides and might do great good.

But Jefferson was not to be persuaded. His mind was bent on retirement. He could not think of launching forth again in a new business or of ever again crossing the Atlantic. Furthermore, he was convinced that more good could be done at home than in France. To all this the president replied that Mr. Jefferson had pressed him to continue in office but refused to do the same himself. Jefferson countered that the case was very different; the president united the confidence of all America and was the only person who did so, whereas his own services were relatively unimportant and could be replaced to equal advantage by a thousand others. He was unduly modest.

The interests of France were now to be energetically supported by their new minister. On April 8, 1793, Citizen Genêt arrived in Charleston to replace de Ternant. He was welcomed by the governor and a large, admiring crowd. His first official undertaking was to commission two privateers to capture and take as prizes any British vessels they encountered. It was on his way to Philadelphia that the French frigate *l'Embuscade,* in which he had crossed the ocean, seized the British vessel *Grange.*

In spite of Jefferson's strong sympathies for France in its struggle with Britain, he would brook no infringement on American neutrality. Accordingly, he condemned in the highest degree the capture of the *Grange* within the jurisdiction of the United States, making it clear to the French minister that the government would take prompt action to liberate the crew and restitute the ship and its cargo. Indeed, he promised effectual measures to prevent equipping and manning vessels in American ports for use against either of the belligerents.

Shortly after this event Jefferson wrote to his friend Madison, saying that cases were arising which were sure to embarrass the United States a little until the line of neutrality was fairly understood by the Americans and the belligerent parties. He continued: "I fear that fair neutrality will prove a disagreeable pill to our friends, though necessary to keep out of the calamities of war."

To no one was it more disagreeable than to Jefferson himself. Again he was caught in the ancient conflict between his heart and his head—his heart beating sympathetically for France and his head recognizing the equal justice of England's case. The people were quick to take sides. He wrote to Monroe (on May 5, 1793), saying that the newspapers from Boston to Charleston were rekindling all the old spirit of 1776. And then, speaking of the French frigate and her prize, he wrote:

"Upon her coming into sight, thousands and thousands of the yeomanry of the city crowded and covered the wharfs. Never before was such a crowd seen there; and when the British colors were seen reversed, and the French flying above them, they burst into peals of exultation. I wish we may be able to repress the spirit of the people within the limits of a fair neutrality."

He ended his letter with this remark, "If we preserve even a sneaking neutrality, we shall be indebted for it to the President, and not to his counsellors."

In the cabinet, Hamilton and John Knox always voted against Jefferson, while John Randolph was divided half-and-half between them. The decision often rested with him, because Jefferson and the president usually voted together. Into this tense balance the new French minister now tried to throw his weight. He opened with fulsome diplomatic reassurances, declaring that his sole purpose was to permit the United States to pursue its happiness and prosperity in peace. But his actions spoke louder than these smooth words. He began by requesting payments on the French debt, not yet due, so that he could purchase provisions and naval stores in the United States. This request, he was notified by the secretary of state, was denied. Genêt's feelings were hurt by the refusal. He became more and more discomfited by the resistance he continued to encounter, thinking that because his country and the United States were bound together by ancient ties of friendship and gratitude for France's stalwart assistance during the American Revolution, he and the French could do what they chose, irrespective of attitudes of neutrality. He now tried to go over the head of Jefferson and to appeal to the president and to the people. The secretary then wrote to Colonel Monroe on June 28, 1793:

"I do not augur well of the mode of conduct of the new French Minister. . . . I am doing everything in my power to moderate the impetuosity of his movements, and to destroy the dangerous opinions which have been excited in him, that the people of the United States will disavow the acts of their Government, and that he has an appeal from the Executive to Congress, and from both to the people."

Genêt could not comprehend that decisions on foreign relations were taken not by Congress but by the president, and this Jefferson tried to make clear to him; but "Genêt's folly and intemperance of language did not diminish." Fortunately, in this affair, the cabinet appears to have acted as a unit. It met by appointment on August 1 to determine what was to be done about Genêt, whose insolence was such as to make further diplomatic relations with him impossible. The entire cabinet, including the president, favored informing him that his recall had been asked for. The meeting was a heated one. Hamilton harangued the members on two occasions about the Genêt affair for three-quarters of an hour each time, and Washington flew into one of his few wild rages directed chiefly at *"that rascal Freneau."*

Five days after this cabinet meeting, the president called on Jefferson at his home on the Schuylkill outside Philadelphia. Washington again expressed his regrets at not having resigned, especially as he was being deserted by those he counted on most; Hamilton had announced his intention to withdraw, and now Jefferson. Where was he to find persons conversant in foreign affairs and with foreign courts? If Jefferson would only continue in office to the end of the new Congress, it would relieve the president considerably. Jefferson, however, expressed great repugnance for public office. He was sick to death of moving in an official circle which bore him peculiar hatred; that is, among wealthy aristocrats, merchants closely connected with England and the *nouveaux riches*. But Washington finally prevailed. After two or three days' deliberation, Jefferson agreed to remain in office until the end of December, and so he wrote the president on August 11, 1793.

The embarrassing affair of Genêt had not yet run its course. Through it all, Jefferson seemed to be trying to protect him from the consequences of his poor judgment and his impetuosity. But Genêt continued in his bull-headed fashion, going over Jefferson's head and the president's and finally appealing to the people, who had much sympathy for him. His efforts failed. His recall was demanded of the French government, which planned to send over three commissioners to arrest him and bring him back to France for punishment. But Genêt elected to remain in America. He married the daughter of Governor George Clinton of New York and settled permanently near Albany as a useful and much-respected American citizen.

One can read between the lines of his letters of the previous spring how much Jefferson longed to return home. In March, he wrote Martha that he had given up his house in Philadelphia and taken a small one on the banks of the Schuylkill to serve him until the time that he could go home. Maria was with him and in tolerable health.

"She passes two or three days a week with me, under the trees, for I never go into the house but at the hour of bed [this letter was dated July 7, 1793]. I never before knew the full value of trees. My house is entirely embosomed in high plane trees, with good grass below; and under them I breakfast, dine, write, read, and receive my company. What would I not give that the trees planted nearest round the house at Monticello were full grown."

He told Martha that his head was full of farming; that he had peaches and Indian corn on the eleventh of July; and that he hoped to cover the garden at Monticello with a heavy coat of manure, because he suspected that the insects which had harassed it were due to the feebleness of the plants, which had in turn been produced by the lean state of the soil.

A month before, he had written Martha, when his head was full of worries about the Genêt affair and the crucial subject of neutrality, these felicitous words: "I sincerely congratulate you on the arrival of the mocking-bird. Learn all the children to venerate it as a superior being in the form of a bird, or as a being which will haunt them if any harm is done to itself or its eggs." *

---

* Although not fearful of being haunted, the author put out a bowlful of raisins for this welcome visitor, who returned to us in Rhode Island, just yesterday, after a summer's absence.

CHAPTER FIFTEEN

❧ ❧

On August 18, 1793, Jefferson wrote Martha, saying, "Maria and I are scoring off the weeks which separate us from you. They wear off slowly, but time is sure though slow." Actually, events in the next few weeks moved rapidly and fiercely. On September first he wrote in a letter to Madison:

"A malignant fever has been generated in the filth on Water Street, which gives great alarm. About seventy people had died of it two days ago, and as many more were ill of it. It has now got into most parts of the city, and is considerably infectious. At first three out of four died, now about one out of three. It comes on with pain in the head, sick stomach, then a little chill, fever, black vomiting and stools, and death from the second to the eighth day. Everybody who can, is flying from the city, and the panic of the country people is likely to add famine to disease. Though becoming less mortal, it is still spreading, and the heat of the weather is very unpropitious. I have withdrawn my daughter from the city, but am obliged to go to it every day myself."

A week later he again wrote to Madison telling him that the yellow fever was on the increase; eleven patients a day had died, and 330 had come down with it; they were much scattered through the town. In the opinion of the physicians there was no possibility of stopping it. No two agreed on the process of cure. Among the victims were Alexander Hamilton and his wife, but they had light cases. In three more days the death rate had mounted to two hundred per week. The president, according to an arrangement made some time previously, had set out for Mount Vernon the day before. Jefferson, however, had to continue his daily trips to the city.

There were few doctors of medicine in town. Some had fled for safety; others had died in the epidemic. One stalwart figure who towered above all for his bravery, if not for his wisdom, was Thomas Jefferson's friend Dr. Benjamin Rush. Between the eighth and fifteenth of September, Dr. Rush had visited and prescribed for between 100 and 120 patients a day, and his pupils between twenty and thirty more. He had lost his mother and his sister, many of his close friends and colleagues and assistants, but he continued his heroic ministrations of bleeding and purging. It is probable that he killed as many patients as he saved. Between the first of August and the ninth of November 1793, a total of 4,044 had died of the disease. By mid-November and the arrival of cold weather, this epidemic had spent itself; but it recurred during the succeeding years, with especial severity in 1797.

Rush was idolized and excoriated for his beliefs and practices. The same Fenno whose *Gazette of the United States* had been so merciless to Jefferson now let loose its tirades against Rush for his fanaticism and his "lunatic system of medicine." Indeed, Rush, as a friend of Jefferson's and a fellow anti-Federalist who had vigorously opposed Hamilton's funding system, was tarred with the same brush as Jefferson. Medical theory and politics became easy bedfellows. Since Hamilton had recovered from yellow fever and had been successfully treated by Dr. Edward Stevens, a boyhood friend from the West Indies whose methods, unlike Rush's, were moderate and conservative, Hamilton joined the swelling ranks of Rush's opponents. He immediately took pains to have Rush's appointment to a chair of medicine in Columbia College blocked. When Rush learned of this, he said, "It is peculiarly gratifying to me to learn that the opposition to my appointment has come from that gentleman."

This statement, though no doubt sincere, has a slight taste of sour grapes about it. Actually, Rush had been pretty nearly ruined financially by the concerted attacks on him. He was deserted by many, and especially by the rich. To be sure, he had won a libel suit against William Cobbett, his most slanderous critic, and was awarded five thousand dollars; but he gave all of the money, beyond the cost of the trial, to charity. Had it not been for the support of John Adams, who appointed him treasurer of the Mint at a salary of twelve hundred dollars a year, Rush would have been without income. Because of his sympathy with the French Revolution, Dr. Rush was called a "French Democrat," which has been likened to calling a New Dealer a Red. Of course, the arch "French Democrat" was Thomas Jefferson himself, and it was he who was really being attacked.

Jefferson had been Dr. Rush's devoted patient and was loyal to him as a friend; but he could never swallow all of his bitter medical theories. Jefferson had little patience with medical theorizing or, indeed, with the medical profession. His thoughts about doctors must have been shaped by the Indian medicine men of his day, who, he said, "inculcate a sanctimonious reverence for the customs of their ancestors; that whatsoever they did, must be done through all time . . . that their duty is to remain as their Creator made them, ignorance being safety, and knowledge full of danger." Like his revered mentor Franklin, Jefferson was a radical empiricist who had no patience with doctrinaire and global hypotheses.

On many occasions in his letters Jefferson expressed his views about medicine and medical men. He saw the good in them as well as the bad. As we have seen, he wrote Edward Jenner congratulating him on his epoch-making discovery of vaccination for smallpox. To Dr. Caspar Wistar, who was professor of anatomy and surgery at the University of Pennsylvania and succeeded Jefferson as president of the American Philosophical Society, he wrote, knowing Wistar to be as opposed as he was himself to excessive blood-letting:

". . . the disorders of the animal body, and the symptoms indicating them, are as various as the elements of which the body is composed. The combinations, too, of these symptoms are so infinitely diversified, that many associations of them appear too rarely to establish a definite disease; and to an unknown disease, there cannot be a known remedy. Here, then, the judicious, the moral, the humane physician should stop. Having been so often a witness to the salutary efforts which nature makes to re-establish the disordered functions, he should rather trust to their action, than hazard the interruption of that, and a greater derangement of the system, by conjectural experiments on a machine so complicated and so unknown as the human body, and a subject so sacred as human life. Or, if the appearance of doing something be necessary to keep alive the hope and spirits of the patient, it should be of the most innocent character. One of the most successful physicians I have ever known, has assured me, that he used more bread pills, drops of colored water, and powders of hickory ashes, than of all other medicines put to-gether. It was certainly a pious fraud. But the adventurous physician goes on, and substitutes presumption for knowledge. From the scanty field of what is known, he launches into the boundless region of what is unknown. He establishes for his guide some fanciful theory of corpuscular attraction, of chemical agency, of mechanical powers, of stimuli, of irritability accumulated or exhausted, of depletion by the lancet and repletion by mercury, or some other ingenious dream, which lets him into all nature's secrets at short hand. [Could he have been thinking of his friend Dr. Rush?]

"On the principle which he thus assumes, he forms his table of nosology, arrays his diseases into families, and extends his curative treatment, by analogy, to all the cases he has thus arbitrarily marshalled together. I have lived myself to see the disciples of Hoffman, Boerhaave, Stahl, Cullen, Brown, succeed one another like the shifting figures of a magic lantern, and their fancies, like the dresses of the annual doll-babies from Paris, becoming, from their novelty, the vogue of the day, and yielding to the next novelty their ephemeral favor. The patient, treated on the fashionable theory, sometimes gets well in spite of the medicine. The medicine, therefore, restored him, and the young doctor receives new courage to proceed in his bold experiments on the lives of his fellow-creatures. . . . It is in this part of medicine that I wish to see a reform, an abandonment of hypothesis for sober facts, the first degree of value set on clinical observation, and the lowest on visionary theories. I would wish the young practitioner, especially, to have impressed on his mind, the real limits of his art, and that when the state of his patient gets beyond these, his office is to be a watchful, but quiet spectator of the operations of nature, giving them fair play by a well-regulated regimen, and by the aid they can derive from the excitement of good spirits and hope in the patient. . . ."

No better statement of a physician's proper role could be made today.

In answer to a letter requesting the history of his physical habits, Jefferson wrote:

"I live so much like other people, that I might refer to ordinary life as the history of my own. Like my friend the Doctor [Rush], I have lived temperately, eating little animal food, and that not as an aliment, so much as a condiment for the vegetables, which constitute my principal diet. I double however, the Doctor's glass and a half of wine, and even treble it with a friend; but halve its effects by drinking the weak wines only. The ardent wines I cannot drink, nor do I use ardent spirits in any form. Malt liquors and cider are my table drinks, and my breakfast, like that also of my friend, is of tea and coffee.

"I have been blest with organs of digestion which accept and concoct, without ever murmuring, whatever the palate chooses to consign to them, and I have not yet lost a tooth by age. . . . My fondness for reading and study revolts me from the drudgery of letter-writing. And a stiff wrist, the consequence of an early dislocation, makes writing both slow and painful. I am not so regular in my sleep as the Doctor says he was, devoting to it from five to eight hours, according as my company or the book I am reading interests me; and I never go to bed without an hour, or half hour's previous reading of something moral, whereon to ruminate in the intervals of sleep. But whether I retire to bed early or late, I rise with the sun. I use spectacles at night, but not necessarily in the day, unless in reading small print. My hearing is distinct in particular conversation, but confused when several voices cross each other, which unfits me for the society of the table. I have been more fortunate than my friend in the article of health. So free from catarrhs that I have not had one, (in the breast, I mean) on an average of eight or ten years through life. I ascribe this exemption partly to the habit of bathing my feet in cold water every morning, for sixty years past. A fever of more than twenty-four hours I have not had above two or three times in my life. A periodical headache has afflicted me occasionally, once, perhaps, in six or eight years, for two or three weeks at a time, which seems now to have left me; and except on a late occasion of indisposition, I enjoy good health; too feeble, indeed to walk much, but riding without fatigue six or eight miles a day, and sometimes thirty or forty. I may end these egotisms, therefore, as I began, by saying that my life has been so much like that of other people that I might say, with Horace, to every one *'nomine mutato, narratur fabule de te'* ('With a change of name, the tale can be told of you')."

CHAPTER SIXTEEN

❧ ❧

Finally released from his duties by Washington, Jefferson reached his home about a fortnight after New Year's Day in 1794. Except for occasional short visits, he had been absent for about eighteen years, and now he looked forward with excitement and satisfaction to retirement from public life amid the delights of his family, his books, and his farm lands. He was fifty years old; his hair had turned gray, but he was erect in posture and retained his elastic step; he kept his habit of regular exercise in all weather. At home with him were Maria, now sixteen, conspicuous for her loveliness, and also Martha and her husband, Thomas Mann Randolph, with their two children, Thomas Jefferson and Ann Carey. Jefferson admired his son-in-law for his warmth and generosity and for his dashing horsemanship, and was so attached to Martha and to his grandchildren that he had persuaded all of them to move into his household and finally to settle there.

He had successfully cut himself off from political life. Since leaving Philadelphia he had seen no newspapers except those of Richmond, and he liked to quote Montaigne's remark that ignorance is the softest pillow on which a man can rest his head. Indeed, he believed that he was thoroughly and permanently weaned from public affairs, regretting nothing except that he had postponed his retirement four years too long. As he wrote to John Adams, who was then vice president: "I return to farming with an ardor which I scarcely knew in my youth, and which has got the better entirely of my love of study. Instead of writing ten or twelve letters a day, which I have been in the habit of doing as a thing in course, I put off answering my letters now, farmer-like, till a rainy day, and then find them sometimes postponed by other necessary occupations." He concluded this letter with the lament that his countrymen were "groaning under the insults of Great Britain," not only to American shipping but to French possessions in the West Indies as well. He clung to the hope that some means would be found of "reconciling our faith and honor with peace." He had seen enough of one war, he said, and never wanted to see another.

In spite of the pastoral calm in which he liked to envelop himself, he was clearly disturbed over the conduct of Britain and alarmed at the prospects of war. He not only loved peace but was also anxious that his country give the world still another useful lesson by showing it other ways of punishing injuries than war. War, he thought, is as much a punishment to the punisher as to the sufferer. He called the British aggressions (his word) wanton and barefaced. Nothing would force the British to do justice but the loud voice of their own people, he said, and this could be aroused only by interfering with their commerce. And then he finally retreated and said that he cherished tranquillity too much to suffer political things to enter his mind at all.

One reason for his turning away from politics was the condition in which he found his land after it had been abandoned to the ravages of overseers for so long. It was far more run down than he had expected. In order to correct this condition, he determined to divide his farm into six fields and to plant rotating crops: first wheat; then corn, potatoes and peas; then rye or wheat; then clover or buckwheat; and, finally, folding in with a buckwheat dressing, or what we call green manure. He calculated it would take him six years to get this plan under way. Time, patience, and perseverance are the only remedy in agriculture, as in politics—so he wrote the president, on May 14, 1794.

After this letter, there was a lull of nearly four months in his correspondence, suggesting that his withdrawal from public concerns was real enough. He was engrossed in "contemplating the 'tranquil growth' of his lucerne (alfalfa) and his potatoes." For the entire year 1794 there are only nine letters in his published correspondence. There have been various interpretations for his silence. Some believed that he was slyly and silently playing politics and mending fences, in preparation for the presidency. We are familiar enough with the "I-do-not-choose-to-run" stance of American politicians. But, in Jefferson's case, one must bear in mind his reluctance to accept public office, in the first instance, and his preference for a quiet, contemplative life. There is no doubt that retirement meant, for him, not a cessation of labor but a shift in his interests from public to private matters and those closer to his heart. In addition, he was hard-pressed financially and had to attend to his personal needs. His retirement from public affairs may also have been another manifestation of his recurrent feelings of depression.

In 1794, according to the land roll, he was in possession of in excess of thirty thousand acres, divided principally between Monticello, Shadwell, Albemarle County, and Poplar Forest. Only a small part of this land was under cultivation; the rest was included in "the range," or pasturage on worn-out, unfenced fields. Jefferson maintained a force of 154 slaves. Both his character and his education revolted against the institution. In his *Notes on Virginia,* he wrote:

"The whole commerce between master and slave is a perpetual exercise of the most boisterous passions, the most unremitting despotism on the one part, and degrading submissions on the other. Our children see this, and learn to imitate it; for man is an imitative animal. . . . The man must be a prodigy who can retain his manners and morals undepraved by such circumstances."

He was caught in the net of what is sometimes called "historical inevitability." He could not manage a plantation without slave labor. If he dismissed his slaves, he would be abandoning them to idleness and starvation. He has been charged with the conviction that the Negro was intellectually and morally inferior to the white. Let him speak in his own defense to these charges. To Benjamin Banneker, a Negro mathematician and astronomer, who had accused him of keeping slaves against his principles, Jefferson wrote:

"No body wishes more than I do to see such people as you exhibit, that nature has given to our black brethren, talents equal to those of the other colors of men, and that appearance of a want of them is owing merely to the degraded condition of their existence, both in Africa & America. I can add with truth, that no body wishes more ardently to see a good system commenced for raising the condition both of their body & mind to what it ought to be, as fast as the imbecility of their present existence, and other circumstances which cannot be neglected, will admit."

He was perfectly aware that slavery not only debased the Negroes but led the whites into shiftless and lazy ways.

Jefferson kept thirty-four horses (eight of them saddle horses), five mules, 249 head of cattle, 390 hogs, and three sheep. His stock was slim for the acreage, in view of the deteriorated state of his land and the fact that no artificial manures were available. He was confronted with the wearisome task of renovating exhausted land and was obliged to draw on other sources of income in order to support his extensive establishment.

In the summer of 1794 he could accomplish little because there had been no plowing the preceding fall, partly for want of horses and partly because of the neglect of his overseers. And in the summer of 1795 he made no progress at all because of illness. From September through November he was confined to his house, this time by an attack of inflammatory rheumatism, and not by a recurrence of his migraine. Both these afflictions, we now know, have a strong psychosomatic component. Rheumatic fever, with hot swollen joints, is in part, at least, an expression of helplessness and may make its appearance when the burdens of life appear to be too great. Jefferson had left the rigors of his official life for what he thought was to be a bucolic retirement. He found himself in straitened circumstances, with inadequate help, poor produce, and empty bins. The stage was set for some sort of protest, but being a man of courage and determination who had made his choice, he could not readily admit discouragement. Instead, his body made the protest for him. One gets the impression that Jefferson, like many vigorous and healthy men, was quick to consider his "constitution sapped" when he felt the effects of some illness. This attack had started the previous month; and when it had somewhat abated, he rode to Poplar Forest, partly to escape the company at Monticello and partly to review his early mathematical studies in order to be able to help his grandson with his school work. To his dismay, he found that he had forgotten much and recovered it with great difficulty. One gets the impression that he felt his powers failing and was again suffering a mild depression; in this setting his rheumatism reappeared, but he was now an older man, with undoubtedly a slight diminution of energy.

Nevertheless, he was still but fifty years old and ordinarily in excellent vigor. By December 1795 he had recovered and was out of doors again. He immediately set about dividing his arable land into regular fields of forty acres each. From his house he could survey nearly every acre of his run-down estate. What he saw could not have pleased him. His overseers had cleared his land in irregularly shaped fields of varying sizes, and these were fenced with snake fences. But soon bushes and weeds grew into the fields, and then more forest had to be cleared and more fences erected. Jefferson did away with the fences and substituted straight rows of peach trees spaced at regular intervals. In December, he planted 1,151 peach trees. This not only improved the appearance of his land but also provided him with the finest fruit warmed on the slopes of Monticello. But it had the disadvantage of making impossible the grazing of any large number of cattle except when his fields were in grass, and this in turn cut down the supply of manure. Furthermore, all his stock ran promiscuously together so that eventually they had to be penned in enclosures and the accumulated manure distributed over the land. He had tried turning in buckwheat as a substitute for dung, but, because of the exhausted soil, his farm book for 1794 showed very meager profits and his bins remained empty.

In spite of this arduous situation, Jefferson could not be tempted back into the cabinet. In September 1794 he wrote John Randolph, his successor as secretary of state, saying that "no circumstances . . . will ever more tempt me to engage in anything public. I thought myself perfectly fixed in this determination when I left Philadelphia, but every day and hour since has added to its inflexibility." He closed this letter with expressions of the warmest sentiments for the president, regretful only at being unable to comply with his every wish. He did not then recognize his own latent wish to be president. He was, however, already waiting in the wings.

Washington strove to maintain the balance of parties in his cabinet, but he had difficulties in filling the posts. He could not move Jefferson, and Madison declined to become secretary of state, though he changed his mind when Jefferson himself was president. John Adams thought that the arrogant influence of Hamilton was enough to keep men from accepting cabinet appointments. And Jefferson was convinced that the Federalists had gained control of Washington, whose memory was already sensibly impaired by age. He found, too, that the "firm tone" of the president's mind was "beginning to relax," his energy to diminish; "a desire for tranquillity had crept on him, and a willingness to let others act, and even think for him."

Although Washington actually had the authority to dismiss any member of the cabinet, such an act would have been unthinkable. In Washington's view, the cabinet was an independent body of executive counselors, and nothing but gross malfeasance could have justified any such maneuver. Hamilton, however, took matters into his own hands and resigned his place as secretary of the treasury on the last day of January 1795, although Washington had repeatedly urged him to continue in office.

While Jefferson was secretary of state, there were rumors that he was ambitious for the presidency. In fact, there had been continued insinuations in the public press to this effect. Jefferson took pains to stamp out the idea in a frank letter to Madison, in which he turned the tables on him and urged him instead to run for the presidency. He said that there was not another person in the United States who could put his mind so completely at rest as Madison if he were "placed at the helm of our affairs." Jefferson's retirement from office was meant for all office, high or low, without exception, he said. He knew his own self and his fellow citizens too well ever to have thought of the presidency; at least so he chose to believe. The suggestion had come from a hostile quarter in order to poison the public mind as to his motives. Every reason which had determined his retirement operated even more strongly against this notion. His health, Jefferson added, was "entirely broken down within the last eight months." His age required that he should straighten out his affairs; they could no longer be neglected. And perhaps the crowning argument was the delight he felt in the society of his family and in his agricultural pursuits. He had no "spice of ambition" left either for his present or his posthumous name; he wished Madison to consider the question forever closed. Above all, he wanted to prevent any division or loss of votes which might have been fatal to the Republican interests. In all these considerations, he painfully felt the loss of Monroe, who was at the moment minister to France. He ended the political portion of his letter to Madison with the disarming statement "I long to see you."

There seems little doubt of Jefferson's candor in pushing aside the thought of his own candidacy either then or in the future, but subsequent events make one doubt the firmness of his decision, or, indeed, how well he knew himself and recognized his deeper aspirations.

It is to be noted that as of Christmastime 1795 Jefferson sent $8.00 to Mr. Benjamin Franklin Bache for a year's subscription to the *Gazette,* being no longer content with the news in his Richmond paper. Nor, judging from his letters, was he content in pastoral isolation. On April 24, 1796, he wrote, in his most colorful style, to Philip Mazzei, the Italian who had come to Virginia before the Revolution for the purpose of cultivating grapes and making wine at Monticello, under the auspices of a company of which Jefferson was a member. Mazzei was now in Florence. Jefferson told him the aspects of American politics had greatly changed since Mazzei left the United States: ". . . an Anglican monarchical and aristocratical party" had sprung up, "whose avowed object" was to convert us to the substance and the forms of the British government, but the main body of American citizens remained "true to their Republican principles"; and this included the whole "landed interest." Opposed to them were the executive, the judiciary, both branches of the legislature, all of the officers of the government, or those who wanted to be officers, and "all timid men who prefer the calm of despotism to the boisterous sea of liberty."

And then he went on in his picturesque manner to say:

"It would give you a fever were I to name to you the apostates who have gone over to these heresies, men who were Samsons in the field and Solomons in the council, but who have had their heads shorn by the harlot England. . . . We have only to awake and snap the Lilliputian cords with which they have been entangling us during the first sleep which succeeded our labors."

Jefferson's letter to Mazzei, with several distortions and mistranslations, finally found its way into the American press. The words "forms of the British Government" were, for example, rendered in the singular as " 'form' of the British Government," suggesting that Washington had turned royalist. This led, for a while at least, to a coolness between the two men, especially as Jefferson, according to his custom, would never rise to his own defense.

In the fall of 1795 and the following spring, Jefferson continued to busy himself with the enlargement and completion of his house and with the improvements to the roads of his estate. He also built a kiln, where he fired brick for his house. In June 1796, the Duke de la Rochefoucault-Liancourt, Lieutenant-General of France, and late president of the National Assembly, but now in exile, arrived at Monticello and remained there for a week. His observations and descriptions of the agricultural practices which Jefferson had introduced are themselves of great interest, especially as they are seen through the eyes of a French aristocrat and man of property. No less interesting are the duke's comments on his host, whom he describes as displaying a mild, easy, and obliging temper, though somewhat cold and reserved.

"His conversation is of the most agreeable kind, and he possesses a stock of information not inferior to that of any other man. In Europe he would hold a distinguished rank among men of letters, and as such he has already appeared there; at present he is employed with activity and perseverance in the management of his farms and buildings; and he orders, directs and pursues in the minutest detail every branch of business relative to them. I found him in the midst of the harvest, from which the scorching heat of the sun does not prevent his attendance. His negroes are nourished, clothed, and treated as well as white servants could be. As he cannot expect any assistance from the two small neighboring towns, every article is made on his farm; his negroes are cabinet-makers, carpenters, masons, bricklayers, smiths, etc. The children he employs in a nail factory, which yields a considerable profit. The young and old negresses spin for the clothing of the rest. He animates them by rewards and distinctions; in fine, his superior mind directs the management of his domestic concerns with the same abilities, activity, and regularity which he evinced in the conduct of public affairs, and which he is calculated to display in every situation of life."

The price of land, according to the duke, was from four to five dollars per acre. Mutton, veal, and lamb sold for fourpence a pound, and beef was to be had only in the winter. A white mason or carpenter or cabinet-maker or smith got from $1.50 to $2.00 a day.

The duke believed that Jefferson's philosophic turn of mind, his love of study, and his excellent library would sustain him if his second daughter, Maria, should marry, and that his future son-in-law would not be able to find any company better than Jefferson's. This was true of his first son-in-law, toward whom he felt all the affection due a son.

November 1796 brought such cold weather that Jefferson lost his entire potato crop by freezing. The new walls of his house were ready for roofing, but building operations were suspended because of the cold. There was also a severe drought. That month ushered in a significant change in his life. The Republican party had settled on him as a candidate for the presidency, quite contrary to his wishes. Washington had declared in his famous farewell address that he would decline re-election. This left the field open between Jefferson and Adams, who was the candidate of the Federalists.

A month later, on December 17, Jefferson wrote a letter to Madison disclaiming any desire to run for the presidency. His own words leave little doubt of his conscious feelings, but one is left with the suspicion that, although perhaps unknown to him, he harbored a deep wish for this honor.

"The first wish of my heart was that you should have been proposed for the administration of the government. On your declining it, I wish anybody rather than myself; and there is nothing I so anxiously hope, as that my name may come out either second or third. . . . I pray you and authorize you fully, to solicit on my behalf that Mr. Adams may be preferred. He has always been my senior, from the commencement of our public life, and the expression of the public will being equal, this circumstance ought to give him the preference."

His letter ended with gloomy forebodings about the country's foreign affairs, and with the remark: "Let those come to the helm who think they can steer clear of the difficulties. I have no confidence in myself for the undertaking." It should be borne in mind that these remarks were "off the record" and written to a close friend. One can hardly believe that it was a matter of indifference to him whether Adams, who was his political adversary, was elected or that he actually favored him—except in a mood of disillusion and fatigue with politics.

As is well known, the candidates for the Federalists were John Adams and Thomas Pinckney; for the Republicans, Thomas Jefferson and Aaron Burr. The electoral college cast seventy-one votes for Adams, sixty-eight for Jefferson, fifty-nine for Pinckney and thirty for Burr. Adams carried all of New England and also New York, New Jersey, and Delaware, with a scattering from Pennsylvania and Maryland, and one vote each from Virginia and South Carolina. Jefferson captured the "solid South," but lost the office by three scattering votes.

On January 1, 1797, Jefferson again wrote Madison, enclosing a letter written to John Adams a few days before and hoping for

Madison's approval or disapproval. Perhaps it was unlike Jefferson to be so uncertain; he had called the vice presidency "the only office in the world, about which I am unable to decide in my own mind whether I had rather have it or not have it. Pride does not enter into the estimate; for I think with the Romans of old, that the general of to-day should be a soldier to-morrow if necessary. But as to Mr. Adams, I can have no feelings which would revolt at . . . a secondary position to him."

In his letter to John Adams, speaking of the election, Jefferson wrote:

"I have never one single moment expected a different issue; and tho' I know I shall not be believed, yet it is not the less true, that I have never wished it. . . . No one, then, will congratulate you with purer disinterestedness than myself. . . . I have no ambition to govern men. It is a painful and thankless office."

For various political considerations, Madison favored changing this letter, and in any event he chose to hold it back. In the background was the figure of Alexander Hamilton, whose enmity for Jefferson aimed at alienating Adams from him. Later Adams was to write of Jefferson:

"With this gentleman I had lived on terms of intimate friendship for five-and-twenty years, had acted with him in dangerous times and arduous conflicts, and always found him assiduous, laborious, and, as far as I could judge, upright and faithful. . . .

"We parted as good friends as we had always lived; but we consulted very little afterwards.

"Party violence soon rendered it impracticable, or at least useless, and this party violence was excited by Hamilton more than any other man.

"I will not take leave of Mr. Jefferson in this place without declaring my opinion that the accusations against him of blind devotion to France, of hostility to England, of hatred of commerce, of partiality and duplicity in his late negotiations with beligerant powers, are without foundation."

On the eighth of February the votes for president and vice president were announced before the two houses of Congress. Vice President Adams proclaimed John Adams and Thomas Jefferson respectively president and vice president of the United States from March 4 next. And then he asked that ". . . the Sovereign of the Universe, the ordainer of civil government on earth for the preservation of liberty, peace and justice among men, enable them both to discharge the duties of those offices with conscientious diligence, punctuality and perseverance!"

This meant a winter's journey for Jefferson, an arduous undertaking for him who had not been seven miles from his home since his retirement, and who abhorred cold weather. He once wrote that he had suffered during his life more from cold than from all other physical causes put together. At the time of his departure it had turned so cold that the ink froze in his pen; but he had to be on hand to preside at a special session of the Senate on the fourth of March. Actually, he had no wish to be part of a ceremony which he sincerely disliked, but he felt that he should be present, if only out of respect for the public. In his view, political office conferred no special privileges and certainly entitled the holder to no unusual respect.

He left home for Philadelphia on February 20, driving his phaeton as far as Alexandria, where he sent his slave Jupiter with the pair of horses back to Monticello. He completed the journey by public mail coach. According to the timetable kept in his pocket account-book, he sent Jupiter and the horses home from Alexandria for $12.00 and left there after dinner on February 23, reaching Baltimore on the twenty-sixth; the fare was $4.75. For $7.00 more he arrived at Philadelphia on March 2.

He begged both Senator Tazewell of Virginia and James Madison to discourage any public reception at Philadelphia, writing to Madison, "If Governor Mifflin should show any symptoms of ceremony, pray contrive to parry them." In spite of his wish to remain in the background, he was met by a military delegation bearing a banner inscribed with

JEFFERSON THE FRIEND OF THE PEOPLE.

CHAPTER SEVENTEEN

❧ ❧

On arriving in Philadelphia, Jefferson immediately called on President Adams at his lodging on Fourth Street, and the next morning Adams returned the call. Jefferson has left an account of this visit. The gist of it was Adams's concern over a rupture with France and the urgent need for an immediate mission to that country. The president recognized that it would be improper to send the vice president and knew quite well that Jefferson would refuse to go. Adams then wished Jefferson to consult Madison, but Jefferson, knowing that Madison had previously declined to go at Washington's behest, held out little hope. Madison was consulted, but declined, and James Monroe was finally sent.

Among Jefferson's first duties was that of presiding over the senate. He had grown rusty on the rules of parliamentary procedure, but as a young lawyer and a member of the legislature of Virginia, he had prepared a *Parliamentary Pocket-book*. This he now revised and expanded, with the aid of his former teacher, George Wythe, into *A Manual of Parliamentary Practice,* which remains to this day the standard book of rules which govern American deliberative bodies. On his way to Philadelphia he took with him not only this *Pocket-book* but, as president of the American Philosophical Society, a trunkful of mastodon bones. His wide-ranging mind could easily encompass both interests.

At eleven in the morning on March 4, 1797, Jefferson was

sworn into office in the Senate chamber. He made a brief address, which concluded with a tribute to President Adams:

"No one more sincerely prays," Jefferson said, "that no accident may call me to the higher and more important functions which the Constitution eventually devolves on this office. These have been justly confided to the eminent character which has preceded me here, whose talents and integrity have been known and revered by me through a long course of years, and have been the foundation of a cordial and uninterrupted friendship between us; and I devoutly pray he may be long preserved for the government, the happiness, and prosperity of our common country."

Let scoffers and skeptics doubt the genuineness of these words, if they will, and insinuate selfish political ambition and duplicity, but the words can also be accepted at their face value.

Having finished his address, Jefferson led the members of the Senate to the House of Representatives, where Adams took the oath of office. Upon leaving the House, Jefferson naturally followed the new president. He stood aside for a moment to permit General Washington to precede him, but, as a private citizen, the general held back and refused to accept precedence over the vice president. The three men departed to the applause of the remaining members.

On Monday, March 6, Adams and Jefferson dined at General Washington's. The two guests rose from the table and left together. As soon as they reached the street, Jefferson told the new president of his negotiation with Madison to have him serve on a mission to France. Adams was obviously embarrassed and started making excuses for not wishing to nominate Madison, after all. When they came to Fifth Street, their roads separated. Jefferson continued down Fifth, but Adams turned off at Market. Of their parting, Jefferson wrote, ". . . we took leave; and he never after that said one word to me on the subject, or ever consulted me as to any measures of the government." Adams was no neophyte in politics. Recognizing the depth of party passions, he doubted whether the Senate would confirm Madison, if he were to appoint him on the mission to France.

Jefferson continued to deny that he had ever had any thought of himself for the presidency or that he had ever exchanged a word with anyone on the subject. He considered the second office "honorable and easy," and the first "but a splendid misery." He was convinced that the Hamiltonians, who were only a little less hostile to Adams than to him, would stop at nothing to alienate the two men from each other. Early in his life he had learned to turn a deaf ear to the many calumnies directed against him. His want of private or public denial of these infamous personal accusations was interpreted by many as further proof of the truth of the charges. For a quarter of a century or more, Jefferson's silence led to many misconceptions about him and served only as a separating wedge between Adams and himself.

After a few days in Philadelphia for the inauguration, Jefferson set out again for home on March 20, arriving there after a week's travel. He wrote Martha, saying:

"The bloom of Monticello is chilled by my solitude. It makes me wish the more that yourself and sister were here to enjoy it. I value the enjoyments of this life only in proportion as you participate in them with me. All other attachments are weakening, and I approach the state of mind when nothing will hold me here but my love for yourself and sister, and the tender connections you have added to me."

Congress was soon to reconvene in a special session, and so Jefferson had to return to Philadelphia. From there he wrote again to Martha:

"When I look to the ineffable pleasure of my family society, I become more and more disgusted with the jealousies, the hatred, and the rancourous and malignant passions of this scene, and lament my having ever again been drawn into public view. Tranquillity is now my object."

He was constantly and repeatedly caught on the horns of this dilemma—between the rancors of active political life and the joys of retirement.

Later he wrote her that her expressions of affection for him were like "gleams of light, to cheer a dreary scene; where envy, hatred, malice, revenge, and all the worst passions of men, are marshalled to make one another as miserable as possible."

The following October Maria was married to her half-cousin John Wayles Eppes—a young man his father-in-law both approved of and admired.

In his account-book is the simple entry on October 13, 1797: ". . . my daughter Maria married this day." Jefferson lost no opportunity for one of his paternal homilies:

"Harmony in the married state is the very first object to be aimed at. Nothing can preserve affections uninterrupted but a firm resolution never to differ in will, and a determination in each to consider the love of the other as of more value than any object whatever on which a wish had been fixed. How light, in fact, is the sacrifice of any other wish when weighed against affections of one with whom we are to pass our whole life!"

He then added some words of wisdom on economy and again on the matter of dress, which from the vantage point of more than 170 years one can only applaud:

"If a debt is once contracted by a farmer, it is never paid but by a sale. The article of dress is perhaps that in which economy is the least to be recommended. It is so important to each to continue to please the other, that the happiness of both requires the most pointed attention to whatever may contribute to it—and the more as time makes greater inroads on our person. Yet, generally, we become slovenly in proportion as personal decay requires the contrary."

Jefferson was doing his best to push forward the completion of Monticello. There were innumerable and exasperating delays. His workmen could not get much done without him, and they were slow even when he was there. Not until the spring of 1799 was the roof completed and the house covered. When the dome was finished is not certain. He had two experienced and skilled joiners and artisans working for him; one of them had also learned stonecutting and plastering. It was not until the second term of his presidency that the house was finally painted, but there remained much to be done on the grounds and in road-building.

There were other things besides domestic details on his mind. The nation's foreign affairs were far from equitable. The fierce storm of the French Revolution was still breaking on American shores, as were the waves of the Franco-British War; and the United States was trying, as it would continue to try many times thereafter, to remain neutral. But American conduct was in fact more pro-British than neutral. The treaty which John Jay had signed with the English allowed them to seize ships sailing to France from American ports. To retaliate, French corsairs began attacking American vessels, and by the middle of 1797 they had seized more than three hundred American ships. This of course aroused heated feelings against the French, and against Jefferson. He was known for his pro-French sentiments and for his ardent and inflexible republicanism, and he became the natural target and butt of the Hamiltonian Federalists, now in control of Congress.

A storm of invective rose against Jefferson. He was accused of moral depravity. In a Fourth of July sermon, Timothy Dwight, the president of Yale, warned of the danger to "our wives and daughters the victims of legal prostitution, soberly dishonored; speciously polluted," if Jefferson were to win the election. Jefferson kept his counsel. He spoke not a word in self-defense. What he did say was this:

"Were I to undertake to answer the calumnies of the newspapers, it would be more than all my own time, and that of 20 aids could effect. For while I should be answering one, twenty new ones would be invented. I have thought it better to trust to the justice of my country-men, that they would judge me by what they *see* of my conduct on the stage where they have placed me. . . ." *

Jefferson had a seasoned politician's sense of timing. He knew how to wait, to bide his time until popular feelings calmed down

---

* The above quotation also appears in Saul K. Padover's excellent book on Thomas Jefferson. In a footnote, the author quotes this parallel statement from that other great democratic president, Abraham Lincoln:

"If I were to try to read, much less answer, all the attacks made on me, this shop might as well be closed for any other business. I do the very best I know how—the very best I can; and I mean to keep doing so until the end. If the end brings me out all right, what is said against me won't amount to anything. If the end brings me out wrong, ten angels swearing I was right would make no difference."

and finally rallied to his support as the natural leader of the democratic forces in the country. He had all the tact and coolness that President Adams lacked and none of the latter's prejudiced impetuosity or reactionary leanings. Perhaps it is odious to compare them, but, of the two, Jefferson was, in modern parlance, far more mature, capable of delaying a present satisfaction for a future good, capable of weighing his own point of view against his adversary's. Adams, on the other hand, was stubborn, dogmatic, and given to passionate prejudices. Among these was his feeling against popular government, and especially against the French Revolution. Yet Adams, if blunt, was always honest. No one could doubt his stand or question his patriotism. It was Jefferson's apparent calm reasonableness and his gift for having others pull his chestnuts out of the fire that often made him suspect.

To the French consul general in Philadelphia, Jefferson said: "Mr. Adams is vain, suspicious, obstinate, excessively egoistic, not taking advice from anyone, and is even still nettled by the preference that has been shown to Franklin at Paris. . . . But his Presidency will last only five years; . . . the whole American [political] system will change with him."

Just why Jefferson wrote *five* years instead of *four* is not quite clear, unless behind his own deliberate calm there was a good deal of impatience for his own turn at the presidency. Being as adept and sophisticated as he was, he recognized the importance of opposition and political parties to the whole business of government. But he looked upon slavish adherence to a party as "the last degradation of a free and moral agent," declaring magnificently, "If I could not go to heaven but with a party, I would not go there at all." He admitted freely that there were upright and conscientious characters on both sides and that a moral and good man was worthy of more esteem than his political tenets.

He had ample experience with opposition to his views. The Federalists under the leadership of Alexander Hamilton were trying to induce the president to declare war on France, but President Adams was more intent on insuring respect for American neutrality than in suffering Americans to be killed. Passions rose until a state of undeclared war on France prevailed, with all the accompanying suspicion, intolerance, and persecution. The French and now the Irish were blamed for the general state of unrest. But the finger of scorn was pointed principally and squarely at Thomas Jefferson.

All this heat and hatred led to the passage of the Alien and Sedition Acts, even while Jefferson was presiding over the Senate. Since these acts were diametrically opposed to all that Jefferson had hoped to achieve in his Bill of Rights, he knew perfectly well that there would be a reaction to this kind of repressive legislation. He kept calm and bided his time. It became generally recognized that he would be a candidate for the presidency and the principal opponent of the Federalists, and champion of true democracy.

In a letter to Elbridge Gerry of Massachusetts, written in January 1799, he expressed his unequivocal views. Here is a portion of his credo:

"I am for freedom of religion, & against all maneuvres to bring about a legal ascendancy of one sect over another; for freedom of the press, & against all violations of the constitution to silence by force & not by reason the complaints or criticisms, just or unjust, of our citizens against the conduct of their agents. . . . To these I will add, that I was a sincere well-wisher to the success of the French revolution, and still wish it may end in the establishment of a free & well-ordered republic; but I have not been insensible under the atrocious depredations they have committed on our commerce. . . . The first object of my heart is my own country. In that is embarked my family, my fortune, & my own existence."

And for this he was willing to fight with all his clear and rational intelligence and, in spite of his former disinclination, to become a candidate for the highest office in the land, to which he actually seems to have aspired for a long time.

CHAPTER EIGHTEEN

❧ ☙

Thomas Jefferson was a staunch upholder of science as opposed to superstition. He also believed in the integrity and independence of the national government and, during 1798 and 1799, spent most of his time spreading his political and philosophical beliefs before the public.

"Let the general government be reduced to foreign concerns only," he said, "and let our affairs be disentangled from those of all other nations, except as to commerce, which the merchants will manage the better the more they are left free to manage for themselves, and our general government may be reduced to a very simple organization, and a very unexpensive one; a few plain duties to be performed by a few servants."

This might be called the distilled essence of Jeffersonian democracy, of which he was the compounder and purveyor. How far we have deviated from his ideal formula everyone knows. In spite of our gigantic complexities and entanglements, this pattern has remained with us to correct our wandering and faltering footsteps, and to prick our national conscience.

Jefferson was at this time entering the political campaign that led to his becoming president. This was no new activity for him; ten years earlier, on his return from France, he had said to his neighbors in Albemarle County, "the will of the majority, the natural law of every society, is the only sure guardian of the rights of man. Perhaps even this may sometimes err; but its errors are honest, solitary, and *short-lived*."

John Adams disagreed with this sentiment, and Alexander Hamilton scoffed at it insultingly. In the heated animosity surrounding him, Jefferson withdrew to Monticello and spent the summer of 1800 busy with his nail factory, with firing bricks for his house, and with overseeing his farms. He kept up his meticulous meteorological records for the Philosophical Society and busied himself with varied other interests congenial to him, as, for example, the use of steam power to pump water for domestic use. At this time he invented the swivel chair, which his enemies said was a device to enable him to look all ways at once.

Perhaps Jefferson withdrew thus from the public eye because of the campaign lies that were beginning to circulate about him. His life had been so upright, open, and continent that it was hard for his political enemies to find good material with which to slander him. They did what politicians have done ever since; they invented falsehoods, or depended on not-too-subtle distortions and innuendoes. First, he was accused of being an inveterate opponent of the Constitution. Next, he was charged with planning to turn "every Federalist out of office," and to destroy the financial systems of the country, "which would of necessity stop all interest payments on the public debt and lead to widespread bankruptcy." The Navy would be dismantled under his command, they said, and free course would be given to privateering; every vessel sailing from American ports would be captured and plundered. The government would no longer be able to pay pensions to the veterans of the Revolutionary War, who, Hamilton said, would be " 'starving in the streets, or living on the cold and precarious supplies of charity.' " Counterfeiting not only would be widespread but would also be practiced with impunity.

There was no end to the calumnies hurled at Jefferson's lofty head. From the pulpit he was charged with robbery and fraud. Among his alleged victims were said to be a widow and her fatherless children, whom he had cheated out of ten thousand pounds left them in their father's will. His enemies spoke of Jefferson's " 'Congo Harem' " and of the " 'yellow' " Jeffersons who swarmed about Monticello. This was the time during which they pointed their prurient fingers at the children of "Dusky Sally," Sally Hemings, the household slave whose offspring were said to resemble the master of Monticello in features and hair color.

Now the religious issue raised its bruised head in the campaign. Both candidates were charged with heterodoxy. Adams even surpassed Jefferson in his aversion to the doctrine of the Trinity, and yet "*he* escaped anathema." Jefferson, however, was denounced as an atheist by none less than Hamilton. One Dr. John Mason, a popular preacher of that day in New York, accused Jefferson of not even believing in a universal deluge. He published a pamphlet, excerpts from Jefferson's *Notes on Virginia*, under the title *A Voice of Warning to Christians on the ensuing Election*. Dr. Mason called Jefferson a profane philosopher and an infidel. " 'Christians!' " he cried, " 'it is thus that a man, whom you are expected to elevate to the chief magistracy, insults yourselves and your Bible!' " In the midst of his impassioned oration, poor Mason had a nosebleed. Undaunted, he continued his attack and, holding his bloody handkerchief aloft, said, " '. . . Send us, if it please Thee, the sword to bathe itself in the blood of our sons; but spare us, Lord God Most Merciful, spare us that curse,—most dreadful of all curses,—an alliance with Napoleon Bonaparte!' " Thus did he invoke and involve Jefferson's well-known Francophile sentiments.

The clergy continued their attacks on him, some reluctantly admitting that he was chaste, temperate, hospitable, affectionate, and frank; but even so he was no Christian. He did not believe in the deluge, they said, and he did not go to church. " 'Shall Thomas Jefferson,' " they asked, " 'who denies the truth of Christianity, and avows the pernicious folly of all religion, be your governor?' " He was not only called an atheist but was accused of aiming at the destruction of the Christian religion. By preference he attended the Unitarian church in Philadelphia, when belonging to that denomination was held in as much opprobrium as being an infidel. The famous preacher and natural philosopher Dr. Joseph Priestley presided at these services. Jefferson felt, as Priestley did, that Christianity was a way of life rather than a philosophical doc-

trine. He would never " 'bow to the shrine of intolerance, or admit
a right of inquiry into the religious opinions of others.' "

But his advocacy of religious freedom did not alienate the vot-
ers of 1800. On the contrary, they were willing to support him
even when he stated, "I am a Christian in the only sense in which
Jesus wished anyone to be,—sincerely attached to his doctrines in
preference to all others."

Jefferson—shy, withdrawn, elegant, and aristocratic—was, in
spite of his fame, personally unknown to the common people;
nevertheless, he had won their hearts and their support; they
trusted him. Although he was no back-slapper, no hand-shaker,
they knew that their cause was his cause and that he would devote
his life to supporting it. Like Abraham Lincoln, with whom he is
often compared, his weapons were words. Jefferson was a master
politician, who deployed his lieutenants, principally Madison and
Monroe, with consummate strategy and enlisted support through
key figures all over the Union. He exploited the press for what it
was worth, in spite of its venality; nor was he above secrecy or
carefully keeping his name out of the propaganda machine. Of
the campaign, he wrote to his son-in-law Jack Eppes that it "will
be as hot as that of Europe, but happily we deal in ink only; they
in blood."

At the height of the campaign, when his name was being be-
smirched and vilified on all sides, Jefferson wrote to his friend Dr.
Benjamin Rush these memorable words, now inscribed on the
Jefferson monument in Washington, D.C.:

*"I have sworn upon the altar of God, eternal hostility against
every form of tyranny over the mind of man."*

But the malicious distortion of Jefferson's character continued.
Hamilton, be it said, in spite of his hatred, announced that he
would support Jefferson against Burr. He wrote of Jefferson in a
letter to the Federalist leader Senator Bayard:

"I admit that his politics are tinctured with fanaticism; that he
is too much in earnest in his democracy . . . ; that he had been a
mischievous enemy to the principal measures of our past administration; that he is crafty and persevering in his object; that he is
not scrupulous about the means of success, nor very mindful of

truth, and that he is a contemptible hypocrite." And yet Hamilton supported him, as did John Adams, who recognized Jefferson as an honest gentleman in spite of his democratic views, but who despised Burr and looked upon him as a "humiliation" to America. There are other views of Burr which present him as a skilful undercover worker, operating from the distance of Albany and being motivated by great personal ambition. Hamilton has called him an "American Cataline." He felt that Jefferson was much to be preferred and had, at least, some pretensions to character.

In the elections of 1800, Jefferson tied with Aaron Burr for first place, each receiving seventy-three votes. They were followed by Adams with sixty-five, C. C. Pinckney with sixty-four, and John Jay with one.

On January 4, 1801, Jefferson wrote to his daughter Maria, saying:

"The election is understood to stand 73, 73, 65, 64. The Federalists were confident at first they could debauch Col. B. [Burr], from his good faith by offering him their vote to be President, and have seriously proposed it to him. His conduct has been honorable and decisive, and greatly embarrasses them."

Burr would not be moved, nor was he willing to electioneer for himself, which Jefferson, however, did effectively and unabashedly; but he was fighting not only for himself but against privilege and monarchism.

Approximately a month later, February 11, 1801, balloting began in the House of Representatives, in an effort to break the deadlock between Jefferson and Burr. Not until more than two weeks had elapsed, and then only after thirty-one hours of voting and the casting of 36 ballots, was a decision finally reached. Thomas Jefferson was declared president and Aaron Burr vice president.

Jefferson's son-in-law John Randolph, Jr., wrote from the Chamber of the House of Representatives on February 17:

"On the thirty-sixth ballot there appeared this day ten States for Thomas Jefferson, four (New England) for A. Burr, and two blank ballots."

So ended the rule of the Federalists—who were fundamentally at variance with and opposed to the republican system. Their chief magistrate, John Adams, has been described as an interesting, eccentric, and picturesque character, like Dr. Johnson, and as unfit for executive office as Johnson would have been. Hamilton, who had become a power behind the throne, remained in some respects an alien in spirit, continuing to fulminate against the new president from the estate which he occupied at 150th Street and what would now be Riverside Drive in New York City.

If Jefferson was a graceful and seemingly self-assured victor, John Adams was a niggardly and unsporting loser. He did all he could to embarrass the new president, filling important judicial posts with eleventh-hour life appointments up to midnight of March 3. Among them John Marshall, the acting secretary of state, a sworn enemy of Jefferson, was elevated to the Supreme Court. Adams had ordered his carriage (so it is said) to be at the door of the White House at midnight and left Washington forever before dawn. It should be added, by way of extenuation, that John Adams was grieving over the death of his son Charles, in peculiarly sad circumstances, in late November. He had every good reason for wanting to hurry from Washington and go home. He found it a special humiliation to witness the success of Burr—to see "this dexterous gentleman rise, like a balloon, filled with inflammable air, over their heads. . . . What a discouragement to all virtuous exertion, and what encouragement to party intrigue, and corruption!" If Jefferson felt as much, he kept it to himself.

On March 4 Jefferson had hoped to ride through the Washington mud in a coach drawn by four full-blooded bays purchased by Jack Eppes at a cost of sixteen hundred dollars in Virginia; but instead he rode on horseback to the Capitol without a single guard or even servant. He dismounted, unassisted, and hung the bridle of his horse on a fence. Another version of his inauguration says that he walked the two blocks from his boardinghouse to the Capitol.

When he entered the Senate chamber, the Republican members rose to welcome Jefferson, who was tall, spare, and plainly dressed in green breeches, gray woolen stockings, and a gray waistcoat. He shook hands with Vice President Burr and then took the oath of office, swearing to uphold and defend the Constitution of the United States. He was sworn in by his distant kinsman John Marshall, the new chief justice of the Supreme Court. The smouldering antipathy that existed between Marshall and Jefferson was happily well-concealed for the moment. Jefferson then began to deliver his now famous inaugural address. It was distinguished for its conciliatory tone and for its sweet reasonableness. Some of its phrases have become part of American history.

After a profession of his faith in freedom of religion, freedom of the press, freedom of the person under the protection of habeas corpus, and trial by jury, to which the wisdom of our sages and the blood of our heroes have been devoted, he closed his inaugural address with these reassuring words:

"I shall often go wrong through defect of judgment. When right, I shall often be thought wrong by those whose positions will not command a view of the whole ground. I ask your indulgence for my own errors, which will never be intentional; and your support against the errors of others, who may condemn what they would not if seen in all its parts. . . . Relying, then, on the patronage of your good will, I advance with obedience to the work, ready to retire from it whenever you become sensible how much better choice it is in your power to make."

When he had finished his short address of about 2,000 words, the new president bowed and left the Senate chamber.

◄§ §►

Jefferson lived another eighteen years. Toward the end of his life he drew a simple design for a monument commemorating what he considered his greatest accomplishments: the building of the University of Virginia, of which he was both founder and architect; the writing of the Virginia Constitution; the drafting of the Declaration of Independence. All three are inscribed on his tombstone. He died on the Fourth of July in 1826.

BIBLIOGRAPHY

◆ᶬᶟ ᶟ◆

The abbreviations used in the Notes for the works listed here appear in
the left-hand column below, opposite the complete bibliographical entry.

Becker   Becker, Carl. *The Declaration of Independence: A Study in
the History of Ideas.* New York: Peter Smith, 1940.

Fam. Lett.   Betts, Edwin Morris, and James Adam Bear, Jr., eds. *The
Family Letters of Thomas Jefferson.* Columbia, Mo.: University of Missouri Press, 1966.

Boyd   Boyd, Julian P., ed. *The Papers of Thomas Jefferson.* 52 vols.
(projected), 18 to date. Princeton, N.J.: Princeton University
Press, 1950–69.

Butterfield   Butterfield, L. H., and H. C. Rice. "Jefferson's Earliest Note
to Maria Cosway, With Some New Facts and Conjectures on
his Broken Wrist." *William and Mary College Series V* (January 1948), 31–32.

Dos Passos   Dos Passos, John. *The Head and Heart of Thomas Jefferson.*
New York: Doubleday, 1954.

Arch. Draw.   Jefferson, Thomas. *Thomas Jefferson's Architectural Drawings.* Compiled and with commentary and a check list by
Frederick Doveton Nichols. Boston: Massachusetts Historical
Society, and Thomas Jefferson Memorial Foundation and
University Press of Virginia, 1961.

Writings   Jefferson, Thomas. *The Writings of Thomas Jefferson, Being
his Autobiography, Correspondence, Reports, Messages, Addresses, and Other Writings, Official and Private.* Edited by

H. A. Washington. 9 vols. Published by the order of the Joint Committee of Congress on the Library. New York: Derby & Jackson, 1859.

Kimball   Kimball, Marie. *Jefferson, the Road to Glory*. 2 vols. New York: Coward-McCann, 1943.

Koch   Koch, Adrienne, and William Peden, eds. *The Life and Selected Writings of Thomas Jefferson*. New York: Random House, 1944.

Malone   Malone, Dumas. *Jefferson and His Time*. 4 vols. Vol. 1, *Jefferson the Virginian*, 1948. Vol. 2, *Jefferson and the Rights of Man*, 1951. Vol. 3, *Jefferson and the Ideal of Liberty*, 1962. Vol. 4, *Jefferson the President*, 1970. Boston: Little, Brown.

Monticello   Bear, James A., Jr., ed. *Jefferson at Monticello*. Charlottesville, Va.: University Press of Virginia, 1967.

Nock   Nock, Albert Jay. *Jefferson*. New York: Harcourt, Brace, 1926.

Comp. Pad.   Padover, Saul K. *The Complete Jefferson*. 16 vols. New York: Tudor Publishing, 1943.

Padover   ———. *Jefferson*. New York: Harcourt, Brace, 1942.

Parton   Parton, James. *Life of Thomas Jefferson*. Boston: James S. Osgood, 1874.

Peterson   Peterson, Merrill D. *The Jefferson Image in the American Mind*. New York Oxford University Press, 1960.

Randall   Randall, Henry S. *The Life of Thomas Jefferson*. 3 vols. New York: Derby & Jackson, 1858.

Randolph   Randolph, Sarah N. *The Domestic Life of Thomas Jefferson*. New York: Harper & Brothers, 1871.

Rossiter   Rossiter, Clinton. *Alexander Hamilton and the Constitution*. New York: Harcourt, Brace, 1964.

Rush   Rush, Benjamin. *Essays, Literary, Moral, and Philosophical*. Philadelphia, 1798.

NOTES

❧ ❧

The numbers preceding each note refer to page and line numbers. The page number precedes the period, and the line number follows it. Examples:

    39.17–40.2: page 39, line 17, through page 40, line 2.
    41.7: page 41, line 7.
    45.6–11: page 45, lines 6 through 11.

CHAPTER ONE

16.36–17.1   *Writings*, vol. 1, pp. 58–59.
17.27   Quoted in Randall, vol. 1, p. 50.
18.21–25   *Writings*, vol. 3, p. 527.
19.15–18   Quoted in Randolph, p. 426.
19.27   Quoted in Randall, vol. 3, p. 542.
22.5–23.22   Koch, p. 4.
24.6–9   Koch, p. xvi.
24.21–37   *Writings*, vol. 1, pp. 397–98.
24.37   Quoted in Nock, p. 14.
25.20–25   *Writings*, vol. 6, p. 62.
26.1–9   Koch, p. 220.
26.9–14   *Ibid.*, pp. 226–27.
26.21–23   *Ibid.*, p. 221.
26.29–27.7   *Ibid.*, p. 333.
27.8–22   *Ibid.*, p. 579.
27.26–27   *Ibid.*, p. 341.
27.37–28.2   *Writings*, vol. 6, p. 269.
28.10–17   Koch, p. 4.
28.29–34   Quoted in Randolph, p. 26.
29.12–23   Randolph, p. 23.

30.7–9   Randall, vol. 1, p. 17.
30.11–16   *Writings*, vol. 6, pp. 348–51.

CHAPTER TWO

31.6   Randall, p. 18.
31.9–12   Quoted in Randall, p. 18.
32.5–16   *Fam. Lett.*, p. 363.
33.2–6   Padover, p. 10.
33.8–10   Padover, p. 15.
33.18–34   *Writings*, vol. 1, pp. 2–3.
34.8–9   Quoted in Randall, p. 220.
34.18   *Writings*, vol. 1, p. 3.
34.20–24   *Ibid.*, vol. 6, p. 411.
34.26–31   *Ibid.*, vol. 7, p. 103.
35.2–7   *Ibid.*, pp. 102–3.
35.10–22   Koch, pp. 363–64.
35.23–25   *Ibid.*, pp. 28–29.
36.24–27   Quoted in Padover, p. 19.
36.31–35   *Writings*, vol. 1, p. 185.
36.37–37.5   *Ibid.*, pp. 186–87.
37.12–14   *Ibid.*, p. 187.
37.27   Randall, vol. 1, p. 24.
38.2–7   *Writings*, vol. 2, p. 238.
39.31–32   *Ibid.*, vol. 1, p. 4.

39.37–40.1 Koch, p. 39.
40.3–13 Quoted in Randall, vol. 1, p. 39.
40.15–36 Quoted *Ibid.*, p. 40.

CHAPTER THREE

42.17–43.8 Parton, p. 85.
43.10–15 Quoted in Parton, p. 93.
43.18–21 Quoted *ibid.*, p. 94.
43.34–44.3 Quoted *ibid.*, p. 97.
44.10–12 Parton, p. 98.
44.16–26 Boyd, vol. 1, p. 33.
44.31–45.1 Padover, p. 26.
45.28–46.14 Quoted in Randall, pp. 61–62.
46.16–28 Kimball, p. 167.
47.12–15 Quoted *ibid.*, p. 174.
47.17–20 Quoted *ibid.*, p. 174.
47.22–27 Quoted *ibid.*, p. 174.
48.6–9 Randolph, pp. 43–44.
48.11–16 Quoted in Randall, vol. 1, p. 63.
49.12–13 *Writings*, vol. 1, p. 196.
49.15–36 Parton, pp. 105–6.
50.4–8 Parton, p. 108.

CHAPTER FOUR

52.3–30 Randall, vol. 1, pp. 68–69.
52.37–53.9 Quoted *ibid.*, p. 75.
53.29–30 Nock, p. 32.
54.13 *Writings*, vol. 1, p. 5.
55.6–19 *Ibid.*, vol. 6, p. 528.
55.28–30 Quoted in Randolph, p. 47.
55.5–13 *Writings*, vol. 1, p. 6.
57.2–8 Randall, vol. 1, p. 98.
57.12–27 *Writings*, vol. 1, p. 122.
57.33–58.7 Quoted in Randall, vol. 1, pp. 101–2.
58.30–59.3 Randall, vol. 1, p. 113.
59.31–60.2 Quoted *ibid.*, pp. 117–18.
60.13–15 *Writings*, vol. 8, p. 363.
60.17–19 *Ibid.*, vol. 1, p. 203.
60.21–25 *Ibid.*, p. 200.

CHAPTER FIVE

61.1–8 Randall, vol. 1, p. 133.
62.16–21 *Writings*, vol. 1, p. 17.
62.30–31 Quoted in Randall, vol. 1, p. 144.
62.34–63.12 Quoted *ibid.*, p. 145.
63.16–18 Quoted *ibid.*
64.2–3 Becker, p. 5.
64.13–23 *Writings*, vol. 1, p. 19.
64.31–36 *Ibid.*, vol. 7, pp. 410–11.
65.15–16 Quoted in Randall, vol. 1, p. 178.

65.17–19 *Writings*, vol. 7, pp. 305–6.
65.21–22 *Ibid.*, vol. 8, p. 500.
65.29–30 Quoted in Randall, vol. 1, p. 180.
65.34–35 *Writings*, vol. 7, p. 126.
65.36–66.2 Quoted in Becker, pp. 24–26.
66.2–8 *Writings*, vol. 7, pp. 304–5.
66.9–19 *Ibid.*, p. 407.
66.20–22 Becker, p. 27.
66.28–35 Randall, vol. 1, p. 179, *n.*1.
67.7–8 Quoted in Parton, p. 192.
67.19–27 Parton, p. 192.

CHAPTER SIX

69.5 Quoted in Randall, vol. 1, p. 196.
69.22–70.13 Quoted in Parton, p. 198.
70.24–25 Quoted in Randall, p. 210, *n.*1.
71.17–20 *Writings*, vol. 1, pp. 40–41.
71.20–23 *Ibid.*, p. 37.
71.23–29 *Ibid.*, p. 41.
72.16–21 Koch, p. 275.
72.24–35 *Ibid.*, p. 277.
72.37–73.5 *Writings*, vol. 1, p. 205.
73.8–9 *Ibid.*, p. 204.
73.25–74.25 Boyd, vol. 2, pp. 237–45.
74.32–75.1 Quoted in Randall, vol. 1, p. 235.
75.18–24 *Writings*, vol. 1, pp. 210–11.
75.33–34 Parton, p. 232.
76.19–22 Quoted *ibid.*, p. 235.
77.2–7 Boyd, vol. 3, pp. 411–12.
77.12–18 *Writings*, vol. 1, pp. 232–33.

CHAPTER SEVEN

81.16–21 Quoted in Randolph, p. 57.
81.28–34 Quoted in Randall, vol. 1, p. 332.
82.14–15 *Writings*, vol. 8, p. 370.
82.31–32 *Ibid.*, vol. 1, p. 312.
83.9–14 Boyd, vol. 6, p. 112.
83.37–84.3 *Ibid.*, p. 136.
84.19–85.3 *Ibid.*, p. 184.
85.21–86.8 Quoted in Randall, vol. 1, p. 382.
86.12–23 Quoted in Boyd, vol. 6, pp. 198–199.
86.26–28 Boyd, p. 203.

87.1–9   Ibid., p. 198.
87.15–24   Quoted in Randall, vol. 1, p. 383.
87n   Iliad, Book 22.

CHAPTER EIGHT

89.16–90.2   Koch, p. 580.
90.7–13   Boyd, vol. 6, p. 202.
90.14–17   Ibid., p. 206.
90.27–30   Writings, vol. 1, p. 322.
90.30–35   Ibid., p. 51.
91.15–93.6   Quoted in Randolph, pp. 69–71.
93.21–34   Writings, vol. 1, pp. 58–59.
94.3–11   Fam. Lett., p. 364.
94.14–31   Quoted in Randolph, pp. 59–60.
95.2–3   Quoted in Parton, p. 276.
95.14–19   Quoted in Padover, p. 122.
95.23–31   Quoted ibid.
96.9–16   Quoted in Parton, pp. 280–81.
96.22–97.3   Parton, pp. 281–282.
97.5–6   Writings, vol. 1, p. 62.
97.19–20   Quoted in Parton, p. 283.
97.25–26   Quoted ibid., p. 284.
98.9   Quoted in Randall, vol. 1, p. 424.
98.32–33   Writings, vol. 1, p. 404.
99.7–11   Quoted in Padover, p. 121.
99.20–31   Writings, vol. 1, p. 444.
99.32–100.6   Ibid., pp. 467–68.
100.7–9   Ibid., p. 444.
100.13–16   Ibid., pp. 394–95.
100.19–22   Quoted in Padover, p. 135.
101.16–102.12   Fam. Lett., pp. 29–31.
102.14–17   Quoted in Randolph, p. 104.
102.24–103.4   Quoted in Padover, p. 129.

CHAPTER NINE

105.8–12   Quoted in Randall, vol. 1, p. 445.
105.20–24   Quoted in Randall, vol. 1, p. 446.
106.6   Randall, p. 448.
106.9–18   Writings, vol. 1, pp. 549–50.
106.26–28   Quoted in Randall, vol. 1, p. 449.
107.7–15   Writings, vol. 2, pp. 7–8.
108.7–13   Quoted in Parton, p. 314.
108.18–24   Butterfield.

108.24   Quoted in Randall, vol. 1, p. 456.
109.9   Malone, vol. 2, p. 71.
110.6   Quoted in Malone, vol. 2, p. 75.
110.18–27   Quoted ibid., p. 73, n.14.
111.12–13   Ibid., Malone, vol. 2, p. 76.
111.17–112.1   Writings, vol. 2, pp. 31–43.
112.15–19   Dos Passos, p. 298.

CHAPTER TEN

113.2–4   Quoted in Randolph, p. 108.
113.7–8   Quoted ibid.
113.15–22   Quoted in Randolph, p. 109.
114.2–9   Randolph, p. 112.
114.10–14   Writings, vol. 9, pp. 313–33.
114.25–26   Arch. Draw., p. 3.
114.37–115.1   Ibid.
115.16–116.3   Fam. Lett., pp. 34–36.
116.6–10   Ibid., p. 35.
116.26–28   Quoted in Randolph, p. 13.
116.31–117.2   Fam. Lett., pp. 36–37.
117.11–18   Writings, vol. 9, p. 340.
117.26–30   Ibid., vol. 2, p. 266.
117.33–35   Padover, p. 148.
118.1–15   Fam. Lett., pp. 41–44.
118.16–30   Writings, vol. 2, pp. 153–54.
119.6–10   Quoted in Randall, vol. 1, p. 480.
119.35–120.1   Quoted in Malone, vol. 2, p. 142.
121.1–4   Writings, vol. 9, p. 378.
121.4–6   Ibid., pp. 380, 381–82.
121.6–16   Ibid., pp. 383–84.

CHAPTER ELEVEN

122.15–18   Comp. Pad., p. 997. See also Writings, vol. 9, pp. 395–96.
123.21–22   Writings, vol. 2, pp. 590–91.
123.29–124.8   Padover, p. 162.
124.11–12   Quoted ibid., p. 166.
124.13–18   Writings, vol. 1, pp. 104–5.
125.5–9   Quoted in Malone, vol. 2, p. 158.
125.18–20   Writings, vol. 2, p. 217.
125.20–22   Ibid., p. 249.
125.22–25   Malone, vol. 2, p. 160.
125.25–27   Writings, vol. 2, p. 256.
125.27–126.10   Ibid., pp. 329–30.

126.10–13   Ibid., p. 332.
126.13–15   Ibid., vol. 3, p. 12.
126.33–127.6   Ibid., vol. 1, p. 107.

CHAPTER TWELVE

128.9–129.31   Quoted in Randolph, pp. 151–52.
130.2–8   Monticello, p. 11.
130.9–19   Ibid., p. 12.
130.22–32   Ibid., pp. 5–23, passim.
131.2–7   Rush, pp. 8–9.
131.15–17   Quoted in Peterson, p. 105.
131.23–28   Writings, vol. 8, p. 384.
132.9   Quoted in Koch, p. 267.
132.11   Quoted ibid., p. 262.
132.17–20   Koch, p. 256.
132.26–133.4   Ibid., p. 257.
133.12–14   Monticello, p. 16.
133.35–37   Writings, vol. 1, p. 108.
134.5–10   Quoted in Malone, vol. 2, p. 248.
134.22–25   Writings, vol. 1, p. 41.
134.29–33   Ibid., vol. 3, p. 125.
135.18–19   Ibid., vol. 1, p. 108.
136.1–8   Ibid., vol. 3, pp. 131–32.
136.11–15   Ibid., p. 133.
136.16–21   Ibid., p. 134.
136.23–29   Ibid., p. 140.
136.32–137.12   Ibid., pp. 218–19.

CHAPTER THIRTEEN

139.13–14   Quoted in Randall, vol. 1, p. 595.
139.16–17   Quoted in Padover, p. 183.
139.30–36   Quoted in Randall, vol. 1, p. 597.
140.13–14   Quoted in Padover, p. 184.
141.1–2   Writings, vol. 9, p. 96.
141.3–6   Ibid., vol. 5, pp. 559–60.
141.13–16   Malone, vol. 2, p. 272.
141.17–142.29   Writings, vol. 6, pp. 286–87.
143.34–35   Randolph, p. 179.
144.4–8   Quoted ibid., p. 184.
144.15–29   Quoted in Dos Passos, p. 373.
144.32–146.3   Quoted in Randolph, pp. 180–81.
146.4–19   Quoted in Padover, p. 190.

CHAPTER FOURTEEN

148.1–3   Quoted in Parton, p. 329.
148.5   Quoted ibid., p. 352.

148.22–23   Quoted ibid., p. 356.
149.3–16   Quoted ibid., p. 369.
149.36–37   Writings, vol. 4, p. 124.
150.9–12   Rossiter, p. 6.
150.25–28   Ibid., p. 9.
150.34–36   Column, April 13, 1943.
151.12–19   Padover, p. 192.
151.28–29   Writings, vol. 3, p. 188.
151.37–152.5   Padover, p. 194.
152.36–153.1   Writings, vol. 3, p. 272.
153.2–3   Quoted in Padover, p. 198.
153.11–27   Randall, vol. 2, pp. 71–73.
153.27–36   Koch, p. 131.
154.7–12   Writings, vol. 9, p. 88.
154.24–25   Peterson, p. 33.
155.4–16   Writings, vol. 3, pp. 363–64.
155.22–25   Quoted in Randall, vol. 2, p. 77.
155.36–156.15   Writings, vol. 3, pp. 459–68.
156.16–24   Quoted in Randall, vol. 2, pp. 83–84.
158.3–10   Writings, vol. 9, p. 121.
158.11–14   Quoted in Randall, vol. 2, p. 92.
159.16–160.9   Quoted in Randolph, pp. 214–15.
160.18–21   Writings, vol. 9, p. 134.
161.35–162.6   Ibid., vol. 3, p. 548.
162.28–34   Ibid., vol. 4, p. 7.
162.37–163.1   Randall, vol. 2, p. 174.
163.2–10   Writings, vol. 9, pp. 162–64.
164.8–14   Fam. Lett., pp. 121–22.
164.23–26   Ibid., p. 120.

CHAPTER FIFTEEN

165.1–3   Fam. Lett., p. 123.
165.6–17   Writings, vol. 4, p. 54.
166.33–35   Rush, p. 795.
167.18–22   Writings, vol. 8, pp. 42–43.
167.27–29   Koch, p. 580.
167.29–169.8   Ibid., pp. 583–84.
169.13–170.16   Ibid., pp. 690–91.

CHAPTER SIXTEEN

171.23–172.12   Writings, vol. 4, pp. 103–4.
172.36–173.2   Ibid., p. 104.
173.17–22   Randall, vol. 2, p. 238.
173.25–30   Writings, vol. 8, p. 403.
174.3–11   Ibid., vol. 3, p. 291.
174.37–175.3   Quoted in Randall, vol. 3, p. 364; Writings, vol. 6, p. 4.

175.36–176.6   *Writings,* vol. 1, pp.
    108–9.
176.15–20   *Ibid.,* vol. 9, p. 99.
176.31–177.18   *Ibid.,* vol. 4, pp.
    116–17.
177.28–178.13   *Ibid.,* pp. 139–40.
178.24–179.28   Quoted in Randall,
    vol. 2, p. 306.
180.4–21   *Writings,* vol. 4, p. 150.
181.3–8   *Ibid.,* pp. 154–55.
181.11–15   Quoted in Randall, vol.
    2, p. 318.
181.21–34   Quoted *ibid.,* p. 324.
182.2–6   Quoted *ibid.,* p. 332.
182.29–30   *Writings,* vol. 4, p. 167.
182.33   Quoted in Randall, vol. 2, p.
    334.

CHAPTER SEVENTEEN

184.3–11   Quoted in Parton, p. 530.
184.31–33   *Writings,* vol. 9, p. 186.
184.37–185.6   *Ibid.,* vol. 4, p. 171.
185.16–22   Quoted in Randolph, p.
    243.
185.26–30   Quoted *ibid.,* p. 245.
185.35–37   Quoted *ibid.,* p. 248.
186.7–24   Quoted *ibid.,* pp. 246–
    47.

187.17–19   Quoted in Padover, p.
    252.
187.22–27   *Writings,* vol. 4, p. 255.
188.16–20   Quoted in Padover, p.
    254.
188.26–29   Quoted *ibid.,* p. 255.
189.17–27   *Writings,* vol. 4, p. 268.

CHAPTER EIGHTEEN

190.6–12   Quoted in Parton, p. 564.
190.22–191.2   Quoted *ibid.,* p. 554.
191.21–193.7   Parton, pp. 568–74.
193.20–22   Quoted in Padover, p.
    469.
193.27–28   *Writings,* vol. 4, p. 336.
193.33–194.1   Quoted in Padover,
    p. 281.
194.5   Quoted *ibid.,* p. 282.
194.8   Quoted in Malone, vol. 3, p.
    500.
194.17–21   *Fam. Lett.,* p. 190.
194.34–37   Quoted in Randolph,
    p. 275.
195.23–26   Quoted in Malone, vol.
    3, p. 500.
196.15–23   *Writings,* vol. 8, p. 5.

INDEX

❧ ❧